Black Ebo

Black Beauty
Anna Sewell
of Queen Vict

Now, nearly a ... phine,
Diana and Chr ... -Thompson tell
the story of three descendants of the famous horse in a trilogy called, collectively, BLACK BEAUTY'S CLAN. Though BLACK EBONY is chronologically the first story, each one is quite complete in itself and can be enjoyed even if you haven't read the other two books.

BLACK BEAUTY'S CLAN:
BLACK EBONY by Josephine Pullein-Thompson
BLACK PRINCESS by Diana Pullein-Thompson
BLACK VELVET by Christine Pullein-Thompson

'I found these books difficult to put down. For those of you who enjoyed Anna Sewell's classic, I can wholeheartedly recommend them.'

Pony Magazine

Anna Sewell's classic, BLACK BEAUTY, is also available in Knight Books.

Foreword

BY BLACK ABBOT

Black Beauty's great-great-great-great nephew

Because of the world-wide interest shown in the autobiography of my kinsman, Black Beauty, I have now taken the liberty of gathering together the life stories written by three other members of my extraordinarily talented family.

These three mildewed manuscripts, the first of which, chronologically, is BLACK EBONY, were found in a loft, in a saddle room medecine cupboard and beneath a pile of rubbish in a deserted loosebox, and, except for the occasional indecipherable word, have been published exactly as they were written.

I have also compiled a simple family tree to help those who wish to know the exact relationship each story-teller bears to our famous kinsman.

Black Ebony

Josephine Pullein-Thompson

Illustrated by Elisabeth Grant

KNIGHT BOOKS
Hodder and Stoughton

First published 1975 by the Brockhampton Press Ltd., as one of the books in a volume entitled BLACK BEAUTY'S CLAN

BLACK EBONY first published by Knight Books 1979

The characters and situations in this book are entirely imaginary and bear no relation to any real person or actual happening.

Printed and bound in Great Britain for Hodder and Stoughton Paperbacks, a division of Hodder and Stoughton Ltd., Mill Road, Dunton Green, Sevenoaks, Kent (Editorial Office: 47 Bedford Square, London, WC1 3DP) by Hunt Barnard Printing Ltd., Aylesbury, Bucks.

ISBN 0 340 23237 4

Contents

BLACK BEAUTY'S CLAN

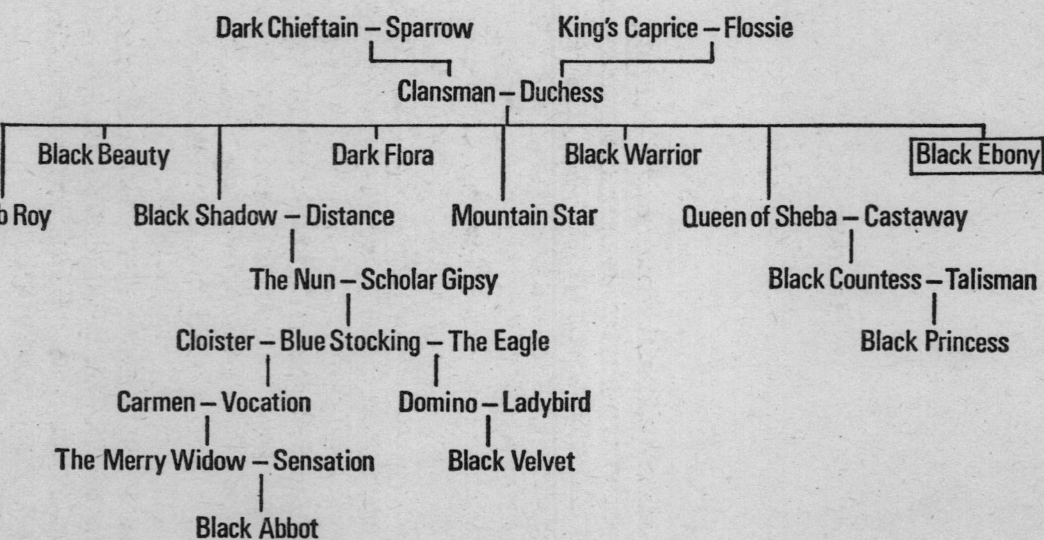

CHAPTER ONE

My foalhood

I did not enjoy being Black Beauty's youngest brother. Our mother, Duchess, had grown very old by the time I arrived; she was rather lame, a little blind and preferred to think about the past rather than the present or the future. Because Rob Roy her eldest foal had died young in a hunting accident, most of her thoughts had centred on her second foal, Black Beauty, and though there had been four fillies and an unsatisfactory colt in between us, it was Black Beauty who was held up as an example of all goodness and elegance and correct behaviour throughout my foalhood. When she talked to the other mares about him he sounded more like a saint than a horse and whenever I misbehaved I was told that Black Beauty would never have *thought* of doing such a thing. I grew to dislike my famous brother very much and I early decided that since I had no hope of rivalling him in goodness I would be as bad as possible and perhaps collect some fame for that.

Farmer Grey's big field was a perfect place to rear foals. There were trees for shade, a large shed in which to shelter from flies or bad weather, a brook for drinking water and a pond for paddling and from which a naughty foal could drive the ducks in wing-flapping hysteria.

I had been named Ebony. The story went that soon after my birth old Farmer Grey and old Daniel, the head horseman on the farm, and Ned his son had been looking me over and they had said, 'Not a white hair on him, he's as black as ebony!' and the name had stuck. My mother always seemed rather disappointed by my lack of white markings. 'Your brother had a very pretty star,' she would say, 'and one neat little white sock.' I never needed to ask which brother, Rob Roy and Black Warrior were rarely mentioned.

There were three middle-aged mares, all old friends of my mother's, turned out with us and I was supposed to play with their foals but they were all younger than I was and less adventurous and I hankered after the company of the yearling cart colts who lived in the adjoining field. I would watch them at their exciting games and hold cheeky conversations with them over the hedge. My mother was always calling me away, 'They are not our class, dear,' she would say. 'You must remember that you are well-bred and high born, your grandfather won the cup at Newmarket two years running.' I didn't care about being high born, I wanted to play rough games, and when I grew older and stronger I found a low place in the hedge and I would jump over and spend a happy hour racing and chasing, biting, rearing and kicking with the much larger but slower and less nimble cart colts, while my mother and her friends stood in a row watching over the hedge and neighing anxiously for me to come back.

My mother was very shocked by this behaviour, but when Farmer Grey learned what I was up to he only laughed and told her, 'You've got a proper little monkey this time, old Pet.' And he always gave me pieces of bread and told me that I would make a fine hunter one day and that Sir Clarence was already inquiring about Duchess's new foal.

My mother disapproved of hunting. She didn't explain to me that it was because Rob Roy had broken a leg and had to be shot, she just grumbled about foolish men who broke their necks and ruined good horses all for the sake of chasing one little fox or hare, so I'm afraid I paid no attention to her but went off to boast to my cart horse friends that I was soon to be a hunter and must practise galloping and leaping.

I never saw hounds until one day in early spring when I was nearly two years old. In the distance we heard this stirring, musical sound. My mother listened and declared it to be the horn and then, as it came nearer, all the horses became very excited and stood with their heads high and ears pricked or galloped round their fields. Suddenly hounds came in view: thirty or forty of them black, brown and white, all giving tongue and behind them came the huntsman blowing his horn and behind him a great many people in scarlet or black coats mounted on fine looking horses.

In a flash I was in with the cart colts, in another flash I was over their hedge and following hounds, so excited by their deep cry and the wild thud of galloping hoofs that I scarcely knew what I was doing. Behind I heard the hedge break and crush beneath the feet of the cart colts as they followed me over.

Some of the riders shouted and cracked whips at us but the pace was too hot and the horses too eager for anyone to stop and drive us back to our field. So we galloped on with them trying to take the fences as they did.

I managed quite well for a time. Watching for a horse ahead to blunder, I would follow taking advantage of a smashed top rail or a battered hedge, but then a hedge with a terrible, dark ditch on the take-off side barred my way. My courage failed me and I refused and in doing so turned across the path of another horse. There was a furious shout from the rider and the stinging cut of a whip across my quarters. I wheeled away and then stopped at a safe distance to watch the huge and beautiful horses striding up full of confidence, and skimming over with the greatest of ease. One day, I told myself, I would leap like that.

The cart colts caught up with me and we milled about confused and all dripping with sweat. The tail end of the field was passing us now and a stout cob whinnied to us. We followed his fat round quarters and docked tail to the corner of the field where he bucked over a small stile.

I raced ahead of the cart colts and flew over after him, there was a crack and the sound of splintering wood as the others followed me. The cob's rider was the same square shape as his horse and he wore a rusty black coat and not a smart scarlet one, but he certainly knew the countryside and cutting across two ploughed fields and through a small wood, he brought us up with hounds again. The pace was still fast and I was getting breathless and tired. My unshod feet were sore and the heavy, clinging plough had slowed me to a weary canter.

The stout cob was fitter and had the staying power of an adult horse. Sadly I watched his quarters grow smaller and smaller. The last stragglers, hounds and horsemen passed me, then the cart colts appeared. 'Let's go 'ome, Eb,' they said. 'Do you know the way?' I didn't, but obviously we couldn't jump back over those fences in cold blood, so we looked for open gates and gaps in hedges and presently, just as the sun was going down, we came to a green lane. We wandered along, stopping to sample the patches of spring grass which had come through in the sheltered corners, for we were now very hungry. Then the lane widened and we saw a group of living carriages or painted wooden houses on wheels. There were two small fires burning and a number of horses and ponies tethered nearby.

We stopped and snorted, but one of the ponies whinnied to us so we went on. Suddenly the shapes of men and boys sprang up silently all around us. I turned in my tracks and tried to flee, but there were gipsies behind us too. One man leaped at me and grabbed my forelock and my ear. Terrified I reared trying to shake him off, but he swung with me, all his weight on my ear and forelock. He hurt me very much and I hated the smell of him and the dark, swarthy face and the rings which dangled from his ears. One hand slid down my nose and he gripped my nostril with a cruel force.

I plunged and reared violently, I struck out with my

forelegs and, still not dislodging him, I reared, higher and higher. He still clung to me and maddened by pain and terror I reared higher still. For a moment I was vertical, then I lost my balance and toppled backwards landing with such force that for a moment I lay stunned.

Then I realised that I was free. There was no hand gripping my ear, no evil smelling fingers in my nostrils, I scrambled up and neighed to the cart colts as I charged the arm-waving, stick-brandishing men who tried to stop me. One stepped right into my path, but I was now so frantic with fear and so determined not to be captured that I would not swerve. My chest knocked him to the ground and I did my best not to tread on him as he sprawled beneath my feet.

I neighed to the colts again as I galloped up the lane, not daring to look behind me. The lane led to a small road and there on a green, surrounded by cottages grazed one of my friends. I stopped beside him. We looked back and neighed, then we listened. There was an answering neigh and presently a lone figure with a wide, white blaize came galloping through the dusk to join us. 'They've got Punch,' he said, 'they've put ropes on him, he can't get away.'

Later we had stopped to graze when we heard the steady clip-clop of a shod horse approaching at the walk and the sound of cart wheels and an old cob came along. The reins were loose on his back and a snoring noise came from the bottom of the cart. 'Drunk again,' he said crossly. 'It's the same every market day. You young fellows lost?'

We fell in beside him and told him our story as we walked along.

'Better come to our place,' he said, 'you'll be safe there and I expect someone will come looking for you by and by.'

So we followed him along the road and up the lane to his farm. We heard the farmer reproached by his son as he was pulled from the cart and supported indoors, we heard the old cob praised as he was unharnessed, watered and fed. We drank at the water trough and then hung about sheepishly waiting for attention and presently the yard gate was shut and we were thrown a couple of armfuls of hay.

We spent a miserable day or two in that farm-yard wondering whether we would ever see our own farm and our lovely fields again and then at last Farmer Grey came with Dick and Ned in the gig and they led us home.

My mother and all the other horses were delighted to have us back safe and sound, but poor Punch never returned.

CHAPTER TWO

My apprenticeship

This episode with the gipsies, followed by the operation which many colts undergo to turn them into geldings, combined to make me far less trusting. For a few months I was very nervous of all strange men, then the memories faded a little but I was never again the same reckless youngster; I knew that cruelty and danger existed.

I would still jump out of my field especially in the spring when the smell of fresh green grass tempted me from the other side of the hedge, but I never wandered far. I still longed to be a hunter, but I had decided to wait until I was old enough to carry a human guide.

The summer I was three years old Farmer Grey sent me to live in the field by the railway line, as he did all his young horses, for this cured any nervousness of trains and enabled them to trot in and out of railway stations all their lives without the least fear.

Then, at four years old, I was broken in. I was very glad to have work to do for I was heartily bored with my uneventful life and longed to be out in the world. I enjoyed learning to go round in a circle on the lunge rein and to walk, trot and canter on command. I didn't object to the saddle but I found the feel of the girth very constricting at first, especially when it was pulled tight, and I made ferocious faces whenever this was done. I hated the bridle straps pressing close round my ears and I did not care overmuch for the feeling of a bit in my mouth.

However, old Daniel and Ned were so kind and patient with me and they praised and petted me so much that I put up with all these discomforts and gradually they became part of the day's routine and eventually I ceased to notice them. Ned was a good rider, very quiet and calm and I felt quite pleased to carry him. At first his extra weight made all my movements awkward and difficult, but, as I grew stronger, I learned to carry his weight as well as my own and regained the feeling of balance and power that I always had when free.

The next hurdle was being shod and this I found very hard to bear. Standing in the forge, endlessly picking up my feet, the smoke and smells, the clank of iron, the hiss of water; the strange feeling of having my feet hammered as the nails were driven in combined to make me very fidgety. I was not a very patient horse and if Ned hadn't been there to comfort me I don't think I could have stood it. Afterwards my feet felt very heavy and cumbersome and made a deafening clip clop on the road, but I became used to it all in time.

The weeks that followed were very happy ones for Ned began to take me out for rides. Sometimes we took messages; to the Mill, to other farmers, to the saddler and harness maker and sometimes we just went where we would. I enjoyed trotting through the woods, talking to the charcoal burner and the woodmen watching the teams of huge horses pull the timber wagons laden with great trees. I enjoyed galloping over commons and fields, climbing to the tops of hills so that we could look over and see what lay on the other side.

Everyone seemed to know Ned and we often stopped to chat to the postman on his pony, the carrier with his horse. In the early mornings we would meet all the donkey carts from the small farms on the hills taking the churns of milk to the station and in the evenings we would meet the horses coming home from their work in the fields, their drills and harrows and ploughs left behind, the ploughman would sit sideways on one horse and lead the other.

I had begun to regard myself as an educated horse ready for the world but I soon found that Farmer Grey thought otherwise and, later on that summer, I was broken to harness. I hated being driven. All those straps; blinkers spoiling my view of the countryside and then, when you had gone through the whole fidgety process of putting the harness on, all you could do was to trot tamely along a road drawing a tiresome trap. You couldn't gallop over fields or wind your way through leafy woods, it was just trotting forever on the hard roads. I kicked at cruppers, I refused to push my head into collars when they were held out to me or to back into the shafts. I sulked and stumbled and went with my ears back whenever I was driven.

Ned laughed at me, but he sympathised and presently he gave up the harness work and started to teach me to jump, or leap as it was often called, and this was much more to my taste. We began over a log and a bundle or two of faggots in the paddock, then we tried hurdles and an old gate. Ned would lean back as we landed but he always let the reins slip through his hands a little so that he never caught my mouth and soon I grew to enjoy jumping with him on my back even more than I did when alone.

One autumn morning Farmer Grey came down to watch.

'Better take him round the farm and put him over a ditch or two,' he told Ned, 'then we'll let him see hounds.'

Ned and I spent some very pleasant days riding round the farm and jumping whatever took our fancy. We began over the small ditches and the low hedges and rails and, as our confidence in each other grew, we jumped higher and higher. Ned had a lot of sense and he would never let me go on until I was tired and began to make mistakes, so, except for the time I refused the brook and tipped him into it and the time I jumped too big and too boldly over a drop and pecked, we had no mishaps or accidents.

At last the day of my first hunt came. We were fed very early and as we ate Blackbird warned me that it would only be cub hunting because the true fox-hunting season does not begin until November the first. But I still set off full of high hopes and Ned, who was looking very spruce in a brown coat and breeches and black boots, gaiters and bowler, seemed cheerful too. The meet was at a remote crossroads deep in the water meadows and I who was obstinately expecting scarlet coats and magnificent horses was bitterly disappointed for only the hunt servants were properly dressed, and even their coats were old and faded, everyone else wore 'ratcatcher', dull browns and greys.

There were a lot of young horses out, many of them much less worldly than I. They stood with bulging eyes snorting at hounds and when we moved off they proceeded crabwise, with wild clatterings of freshly shod hoofs.

Most of the riders looked like farmers, but there were a good many grooms and nagsmen out on young horses, a fair number of children, especially boys, a sprinkling of ladies and gentlemen and two or three soldiers.

'Going to draw the osiers, I shouldn't wonder,' said the old grey horse I fell in beside as we clattered down the road. The horsemen spread out and surrounded the marshy osier bed as hounds were put in and I, who had imagined an immediate chase and seen myself leaping hedge and ditch and gate, grew more and more disappointed as time passed and nothing happened. Ned and the rider of the old grey were discussing the corn harvest and banging the crooks of

their hunting whips against their saddles. They gave cries of encouragement to the young hounds when they came out of the osiers and stood looking about them aimlessly or sat down for a good scratch.

At last the old hounds picked up a scent and the deep sound of their voices echoed up and down the osier bed, but there was still no action; Ned walked me round for a little and the old grey horse told me that cub hunting was usually like this for its whole purpose was to teach young hounds to hunt, and to stir up the fox cubs so that they would leave the family home.

Presently the sun became hot and the old horse slept, until a fox cub peeped out of the undergrowth and there was a burst of crop-banging and shouts of 'Tally-ho bike!' But still no action.

Later we rode on to a small wood, hounds were put in and we went through the whole procedure again, even to the old grey horse falling asleep. Then Ned said that he had work to do and we must go home.

As I ate my second breakfast I grumbled to Blackbird about the unexciting nature of my hunt.

'You don't realise how lucky you are to be taken out quietly like that,' he told me. 'I've known young horses ruined by hard riding. Taken on a fast hunt, galloped nearly to death, broken winded and lame before they'd reached their full strength. And I've known others so over-excited by their first hunt that they could never be calm again, but were always lathered with sweat, sidling, jogging, fighting with their riders from the moment they saw hounds till the time they got home.'

In the afternoon when Ned was grooming me

Farmer Grey came into the stable. 'Sir Clarence's man has just been round,' he said. 'They saw Ebony out this morning and were very much struck with him. Sir Clarence is coming over himself in a day or two to try him.'

Ned took the news coldly. 'They'll hunt him to death before he's five.'

'I reminded Sir Clarence that the horse was only five next time and he said that he intended to keep him for his own second horse this season and he would take care not to overdo him.'

'So long as he don't let that dolt Roger ride him,' said Ned.

'I think he's intended for the young ladies,' answered Farmer Grey. 'He'll make a beautiful horse for a lady in a year or two.'

'Miss Fanny's all right, the other two aren't up to much,' complained Ned,

'Sounds as though you'll soon be off,' said Blackbird when we were alone together again.

Sir Clarence came to try me. Having only had Ned on my back before, I hardly knew how to behave with an unfamiliar rider but Sir Clarence gave much the same signals; he was slower and stiffer than Ned, but equally quiet and patient and I could tell he was a rider to respect. He tried me out thoroughly at the walk, trot and canter, then we had a gallop right round a stubble field and then he put me over several fences. Ned took me when he dismounted.

'He's still a little green,' said Sir Clarence patting me, 'but my word he can gallop and he's got a powerful leap.'

'Yes, jumps like a stag,' agreed Farmer Grey

proudly. 'Now come along to the house, Sir Clarence, and try a glass of Mrs. Grey's sloe gin.'

'I'm going to miss you Eb,' said Ned sadly. I nibbled his coat lapel trying to explain that I was going to miss him too. Slowly we walked back to the stable.

Next day I was clipped. Farmer Grey told Ned that Sir Clarence had asked for it to be done, because he felt it was too much to ask of a young horse that he should be clipped by complete strangers. And as I felt those tickling clippers creeping over my body I felt sure that I would have kicked any stranger who treated me so. But since it was Ned I accepted it all as a necessary evil and only showed him with a lifted hoof or a ferocious face when the blades grew too warm or began to pull. Then we would stop and give poor red-faced Dick, who was turning the handle of the machine, a rest while Ned oiled the blades.

'If you ask me it's downright unnatural,' Dick complained. 'They wouldn't have coats if they didn't need them, so why take it off?'

'The speed they go hunting is unnatural too,' Ned told him. 'My Father has told me that fifty years ago when they first bred the fast hounds we have today, many good horses foundered and died. Many of the gentlemen would boast about how many horses had died under them and a lot of it was due to the thick coats. But people didn't take to clipping for a goodish while because they thought it made the horses die young and some said it made them blind. Of course we know that none of that's true.'

CHAPTER THREE

My life at Earleigh Court

Sir Clarence's establishment, Earleigh Court, was very much larger and more handsome than the farm. The stables were entered through an archway with a clock tower above and a clock that chimed every hour. The yard was gravelled with a plot of grass in the centre and the gravel was always kept raked perfectly smooth and without a wisp of hay or straw in sight. The stables, the carriage houses and the harness rooms stood all round the yard and above them were lofts where the hay and straw was kept and the rooms for the young grooms; the older, married grooms and the coachman all had cottages nearby.

My stable was a very large loose box, well bedded down with the best wheat straw. One side of it was taken up with an iron manger and hayrack, there were green tiles above the manger and the hayrack was a low one so that I could eat in comfort. The walls and door were of brown varnished wood with iron railings above me so that I could see out on three sides but I couldn't put my head out or bite the horse next door.

When I had been rugged up in very smart rugs and Ned had left me I took a sip of water, snatched a mouthful of hay and roamed restlessly round my box. Then, missing Ned and Blackbird, I gave a loud neigh. A very wellbred chestnut head looked at me through the iron bars. 'Kindly moderate your neighs,' it said, 'that noise is deafening. My name is Estella, by Starlight; I imagine you've come to take the place of Patience; she went lame.'

I explained who I was and said that I understood that I was to be Sir Clarence's second horse as it would be my first season's hunting. She told me that four horses, Merlin, Bayard, Sultan and Nimrod were out hunting, but that two should be back at any moment and then returned to her hayrack.

At three o'clock Merlin, an enormous grey of almost seventeen hands was led into the box on the other side of me and Bayard, a sixteen-two bay was taken into the box beyond Estella. Rugs were flung on and they were offered buckets of warm gruel.

'These are the first horses,' Estella explained to me. 'Sir Clarence and Mr. Roger have changed to fresh horses and gone on hunting while Pat and Bert brought the tired ones home.'

'They weren't as fresh as usual,' said Merlin. 'All the second horsemen lost us, they didn't come until very late and they'd covered a mile or two by the look of them.'

'Nothing to what we'd covered,' groaned Bayard when he'd sucked down a mouthful or two of gruel. 'There was a very fast thing in the morning. We found and he made a straight line for the hills. They killed in a quarry and Mr. Roger was very peeved because he wasn't up, but it was his own fault he was coffee-housing – chattering to his friends – when they found and got a bad start, then he expected me to catch the leaders and I just couldn't do it. Then we found again at Fitton Oaks and this one ran towards the river, field after field of water-logged plough and do you think Mr. Roger can tell ridge from furrow, not him! No headlands for him either. Straight through the deepest going and no thought of a breather before he rams you at some great bull-finch. I was nearly down several times; he just doesn't give you a chance.'

'Poor old Bayard,' said Estella sympathetically. 'Now Sir Clarence is always so thoughtful. He picks a wide, water-filled furrow whenever he can. He knows that if a furrow holds water it must have a hard bottom and so will be much less tiring for a horse than deep, muddy going.'

'I wish he'd knock some sense into that son of his,' grumbled Bayard. 'I'm quite pumped out. Too tired to eat a thing and so hot, it's stifling under these rugs.'

Bert and Pat came back then having changed into their stable clothes and began to groom the tired and dirty hunters hissing through their teeth as they worked.

'Bayard's broken out,' Pat called, 'What's Merlin like?'

'Dry as a bone,' answered Bert, knocking his curry comb out on the floor.

Presently Pat fetched Mr. Johnson the stud groom to have a look at poor Bayard and they stood discussing his exhausted and feverish state and the cold sweat he'd broken out into. Then Mr. Johnson went off to get what he called a 'pick me up'.

'Beer, I expect,' said Estella.

The activity in the stable suddenly increased. Lanterns appeared everywhere and as well as the returned hunters being groomed, rugged up and bandaged, Estella and I were being attended to. A small stable boy came into my box with a skip and pitch fork and soon straightened and tidied my straw. My water was changed, my hayrack replenished. Then there were hoofs in the yard, 'Sultan and Nimrod,' said Estella neighing a welcome. I heard Sir Clarence's voice and then a louder less pleasing voice ordering the dog cart to be brought round in an hour to take him to the station.

Sir Clarence came into the stable and looked at Bayard and Merlin and then at me. He was very dirty too, all his fine clothes covered in mud. He had Bert and Mr. Johnson with him when he came into my box and Bert had my headcollar on and my rugs off in a flash.

'Not at all a bad-looking animal,' said Mr. Johnson as they stood considering me, 'in time he should make up into something very nice indeed. Pity he isn't a hand taller.'

Sir Clarence laughed, 'Never mind he'll make a perfect hunter for Miss Fanny and I think he'll just about carry me; I don't ride as hard as I used to – growing old. The lad at the farm made quite a good job of clipping him.'

'Yes, except for the whiskers, I do hate to see a lot of untidy whiskers on a well-turned out horse,' said Mr. Johnson and when Sir Clarence had gone he produced a pair of scissors from his pocket and gently clipped all mine away.

It wasn't until we were fed and settled for the night and the grooms took their lanterns and went away that I began to regret my loss; I'd never realised how useful whiskers are. It was difficult to find my way around a strange stable in the dark, for they feel out the bucket and hayrack for you and save you from banging your nose.

Estella and I talked again when we'd finished our feeds. Bayard still felt done up and was lying down, Merlin was munching hay too busily for conversation and I think she was pleased to have someone to instruct in the way of life at Earleigh Court.

She told me that Mr. Johnson was an excellent stud groom and really knew his job, that Pat who did her, Bayard and Jupiter, was very good and careful and took a great pride in her appearaace, but that Bert who would be doing me as well as Merlin and Nimrod, was careless and rough. Mr. Johnson had to be after him all the time and he'd given her a girth gall once by carelessly pinching her skin when he saddled her. As for rollers he always pulled them up far too tight. Poor Patience had often stood in discomfort all night long because when he rugged her up he'd pulled the roller too tight to permit her to lie down.

'Blow yourself out,' she advised. 'Whenever he does up the roller take a deep breath and hold it, then, when you let the breath go, you'll find the roller comfortably loose, it's the only way.'

'He's not so bad,' Merlin told me slowly and calmly. 'Estella's so thin-skinned and sensitive and she's always had an easy life. I had a really bad groom once, he didn't clean the water bucket for months and he left a dead mouse in my manger for a week and never bothered to investigate why I wasn't eating up; just went on tipping more feed on top of it.'

I soon settled down in my new house though I missed Ned and Blackbird, and most of all, my rides with Ned.

Our stables were kept extremely clean and tidy for, as well as being throughly mucked out every morning, small stable boys ran in and out with skips all day long. We were groomed and groomed, and the food was excellent.

We were exercised in a body under Mr. Johnson's watchful eye, each groom riding one horse and leading another and this crocodile of horses would trot solemnly round the roads and lanes nearly always taking the same route. At a certain spot those horses that were already fit and working quite hard would return home and I who was considered unfit, a carriage horse who had developed a sore shoulder and so had to be ridden rather than driven, and the two luckless horses that were to carry Miss Grace and Miss Griselda later in the day and so must be thoroughly tired out, went on for another three or four miles.

I enjoyed the companionship of this crowd of horses and the noise of so many hoofs was inspiring, but taking the same way time after time was very monotonous and there seemed to be no chance of a canter or gallop, though we passed many an inviting stretch of turf.

Then Mr. Johnson began to ride me when he escorted the young ladies for their almost daily ride, but this too was frustrating. Miss Grace was nervous. She was the youngest of the three sisters and had pale fair hair and eye lashes and weak-looking pale blue eyes. Miss Griselda, the middle one, was a lump with no aptitude for riding. This was not her fault, but her boundless self-confidence and her habit of grumbling at her horse and blaming him for her own shortcomings, irritated us all. Miss Fanny was slim and long-legged and high-spirited and always demanding a gallop or a jump, so she would be skimming over sheep hurdles on Estella, Miss Griselda would make a half-hearted attempt to follow and belabour poor Bayard for refusing while Miss Grace sobbing with terror would plead pitifully with Mr. Johnson not to make her canter. I did my best to behave. I stayed close beside Juno so that Mr. Johnson could grab Miss Grace's reins whenever it was needed, I opened and shut gates nearly, but I did find it hard to remain at a sedate walk while Estella galloped and jumped, and

even the smallest prance of protest brought a wail of fear from Miss Grace and an angry rebuke from Mr. Johnson.

At last I was considered fit to hunt and this did enliven my life. Sir Clarence wasn't bold enough for my taste, but I supposed that he was getting on in years and no longer fell lightly and this cramped his style.

Merlin and Bayard never tired of telling me that I was a hot-head and needed a steady rider. 'Left to your own devices you would have broken your neck a hundred times over,' they told me. And, hacking home after a particularly fast run, Bayard began to lecture me again. 'You're so wild, Ebony. You *never* look before you leap, I know you are only a four-year-old, but we value Sir Clarence and we don't want a good master killed because a youngster can't resist showing off.'

'I once saw a horse land on a harrow, a spiked harrow,' said Estella. 'Farmers just leave these dangerous things lying under hedges, they never think that we may land among the chains and spikes, falling or damaging our legs and feet for life.'

I was reared in Ireland,' Bayard told us, 'and there you find every sort of rubbish in the hedges and ditches and often a fine fat pig asleep on the landing side of a bank! But there the riders are pretty circumspect, they jump more in the old fashioned way, the way they rode before the Leicestershire style and the flying leap, and the horses hold themselves ready to make a sudden extra effort should they see something waiting to trap them. You wouldn't do there, Ebony.'

However, despite the fears of my stable companions, I finished the season without mishap. Looking back, I can see that this was chiefly due to Sir Clarence's restraining hand, but I was too young and cocksure to believe it at the time.

Hunting ended on April the first and they immediately began to rough us off. During the next month our oats, exercise and rugs were gradually reduced and then some of the horses had their shoes off and some were re-shod with grass tips. Then in May the first hunters were led away in a long string to the fields where they were to spend their holidays. As I watched Merlin and Bayard and Estella deserting me I neighed loudly and indignantly and dashed myself against the walls and bars of my stable in an attempt to follow.

Juno, the little cob, was hastily moved into Estella's box to keep me company. 'No you can't have a holiday, Ebony,' said the small stable boy who brought her. 'You've only just started work and Sir Clarence says you have a lot to learn before you are fit to carry Miss Fanny.'

The yard was much quieter now that hunting was over, though of course there were carriage horses in the stable opposite, but two pairs of them had gone to London with the family so most of the activity we saw was the spring cleaning and painting of the stables.

I enjoyed Juno's company. I had grown fond of Estella, but she thought too much about herself to be a really interesting companion, she was always wanting her mane admired, or bemoaning some nearly invisible swelling in her fetlock or complaining of the dull shade her chestnut coat became when she was clipped. Juno was hogged and docked so she was very glad that she was not to be turned out for the summer and left to the mercy of the flies, who tormented her terribly. She had changed hands several times in her life and so had many interesting stories to tell about her other places, but she was such a steady, useful animal that she was always in demand to take messages here, there and everywhere and then I was left on my own.

However I had acquired another friend. A small black cat had jumped down into my loose box one day and spent hours attentively watching a mousehole under my manger. He didn't catch the mouse, but he told me his name was Sambo. He liked my stable and I liked the way he purred and rubbed himself against my face as he marched up and down the edge of my hayrack and manger so we quickly became fast friends and whenever he felt like a nap or a chat he would come to see me.

Mr. Johnson rode me almost every day. He would take me in the park and make me practise circling and stopping and starting and cantering with each leg leading in turn. Then he took to riding me in a side-saddle, which felt very strange at first and not nearly so comfortable as having one of the rider's legs on each side to keep you balanced and give signals. I soon learned that a tap with the whip gave the signal on the legless side, but I could not understand why I must now always canter with the off fore leading and straight from the walk without any trotting in between. Juno explained it to me. She said that it was very jolting for the lady if a horse cantered with the near fore, as that was the side she was sitting on, and trotting fast was very jolting too, so ladies' horses were taught to canter straight from the walk and were generally much more carefully trained than gentlemen's horses.

By the time that the family came back from London, Mr. Johnson was able to tell Sir Clarence that I was now a suitable mount for Miss Fanny.

There followed a very happy time. Miss Fanny rode me almost every day and seemed delighted with me. Her sisters had given up until a more satisfactory mount could be found for Miss Griselda and, as it was not considered correct or safe for a young lady to ride alone, Mr. Johnson or another of the older grooms, riding one of the carriage horses, always accompanied us. Mr. Johnson was much more adventurous when not weighed down by the responsibility of timid riders or a long string of valuable hunters and we were allowed long, fast gallops and quite a few jumps. Miss Fanny and I were always on the look out for suitable hedges and brooks, we found stiles and timber and once a five barred gate though Mr. Johnson disapproved of this.

For me it was as though I had Ned again. We would see a tempting stretch of turf or a conveniently placed fence at the same moment and know each other's mind. When ridden by Sir Clarence or Mr. Johnson I was a horse taking orders, but Miss Fanny and I were partners, sharing the same excitements, planning, sometimes even plotting together.

Though I missed the freedom of the fields these rides, the freshly cut bundle of grass that was brought me daily and the company of my cat kept me contented. Sambo and I often played together and it was considered one of the sights of the stable to see the whole of his tail disappear into my mouth while he purred happily, Miss Grace, being of nervous disposition always screamed. I would push him about with my nose making ferocious faces and he, pretending to be equally angry, would slap my face with his paws, always keeping his claws carefully sheathed. He often slept on my back, comfortable and warm on my summer rug, and then I had to move with great caution to avoid throwing him off.

CHAPTER FOUR

A good horse ruined

The summer passed, the other hunters were brought up from grass, fat, sleepy and rather dull. Grooming, exercising and ever-increasing oat rations began again, but this year I was the fittest horse in the stable. Estella was back in the next box, rather jealous that I had become such a favourite with Miss Fanny and already bemoaning the fact that her beautiful golden coat would soon be shaved away by the clipping machine.

That season I became an experienced hunter. I carried Sir Clarence for several weeks, generally as his first horse, and then he decided that I was behaving in a manner so much more temperate that Miss Fanny would be safe with me.

We were both delighted. She was so light and easy to carry and with the two of us watching to see which way hounds broke we rarely got a bad start. This, with our fondness for jumping, meant that we were always well up and we soon made a name for ourselves. There was the famous occasion of the five mile point from Crowley's Gorse to Austin's Mill spinney when only the huntsman, one very hard-riding squire and Miss Fanny were up and everyone else, including Sir Clarence, had been stopped by the swollen state of the Beverley brook.

Sir Clarence was rather proud of his daughter's riding, but Mr. Roger seemed to be jealous and was always making unkind remarks, saying that it was unfeminine to ride hard, that she would never get a husband, that any lady who rode too well became laughing stock in the men's clubs.

Happiness, though pleasant to experience, is dull to read about. I could tell of endless hunts, of hundreds of fences jumped without mishap, of a few falls, of spring and autumn rides of summer holidays fetlock deep in grass, of getting fit and of being roughed off. Enough to say that the seasons passed. That I filled out and became rather more handsome and a great deal more sensible. That Miss Fanny grew up and became beautiful. That Sambo also grew larger and more magnificent and we were such fast friends that sometimes the lads would move me to another loose box just to tease him and then listen laughing to Sam's loud miaows and my answering whinneys until we found each other again.

There were some less happy events. Bayard became touched in the wind and was sold for light work, Estella's elegant legs began to give trouble so it was decided that she should stop work and have a foal and she disappeared to the farm. Bert left to work on the railway and Ben who had been one of the little stable boys was promoted to his place.

Ben's story was a sad one. He had no parents and no relations that he'd ever heard of and was found, ragged and barefoot, living on rubbish from a market and sleeping in a ruined building with a gang of homeless boys, all huddled together for warmth, by the famous Dr. Barnardo who started so many homes for starving boys and girls. Sir Clarence, who was a great supporter of this work, hearing that there was a boy who wished to work with horses had found him a family on the estate and taken him on as stable boy. It had turned out a great success for Ben loved horses and we loved him. And, though he never grew very tall, through having been so starved in childhood, he had a nice, kind, freckled face and was always lively and good-humoured.

So four years passed and it seemed to me that Earleigh Court was the world, and happiness the natural state of things. The first blow fell suddenly; we heard that Lady Hilton was ill and must spend the winter in a warmer climate and that Miss Fanny would go with her.

Miss Fanny came to tell me about it herself. She cried a little as she told me how much she was going to miss our hunting. 'But it's only for a few months, Ebony,' she promised me, 'I shall be back in the spring.'

There was a subdued feeling in the stables all the next week and no hunting. But, once Lady Hilton and Miss Fanny had left with Sir Clarence, who was going to settle them in and then return, Mr. Roger appeared and began to lord it over everyone. He had grown into a stout young man of twenty-four with a loud, fruity voice and a pompous and sometimes overbearing manner. He was disliked by both grooms and horses so I was not at all pleased at hearing him order me for the meet next day. 'Ebony and Sultan,' he said, 'and I shall ride Ebony first. Send a lad up with them and I'll take the dog cart.'

'Now Sir, you know that Ebony isn't really up to your weight,' said Mr. Johnson respectfully. 'Sir Clarence was always careful not to give him a hard day when he rode him; it would break Miss Fanny's heart if any harm came to that horse.'

'If you think he's going to spend the whole winter eating his head off in idleness you're very much mistaken,' Mr. Roger spoke rudely, 'He must take his turn with the rest and, since Miss Fanny is abroad, her feelings are neither here nor there.'

'Very well, sir,' said Mr. Johnson coldly.

So next day Ben rode Sultan and led me over to Catterick Park. We went slowly but arrived early and stood in the drive outside the large plain house watching the other arrivals. The hunters were mostly ridden up by grooms, the gentlemen came on their covert hacks or in their dog carts. Country house parties came in carriages or wagonettes and the ladies who had come to watch drove up in elegant phaetons and carriages of every description.

It was a lawn meet, which meant that there was a party indoors and menservants came round with drinks and sandwiches for those outside. Ben had a glass of ale and seemed pleased with it. At last Mr. Roger raced up in our dog cart, he threw the reins to the groom sitting behind him and strode into the house.

'Oh dear, why doesn't he allow more time?' gasped poor Shamrock who was dripping with sweat. 'We waited at the front door for twenty minutes getting thoroughly chilled and then we came here at such a pace, uphill and downhill, I haven't drawn breath all the way.'

Presently the riders began to come out of the house and the grooms pulled off rugs and tightened girths. Everyone was mounting but there was no sign of Mr. Roger. I fidgeted impatiently. At last he came, his face was redder than ever, 'Cherry brandy,' said Sultan sniffing.

Hounds were moving off. I sidled and pranced in an agony of impatience for I could see that we were going to be left behind. Mr. Roger swore at me and then at Ben who was trying to hold me still. Even when he was up he was fiddling with his whip and gloves. I snatched at the reins and when he jerked my mouth in retaliation I gave a small protesting rear. At last he let me go and I hurried forward making my way through the press of horses to what I thought of as my rightful place, the front.

We caught up at covertside and I watched, trembling with excitement, as hounds waded through the undergrowth, their sterns lashing as they found faint traces of fox. At any moment their deep cry would resound through the wood, the huntsman would blow his horn and we would be off across country taking hedge and fence and ditch as they came. Miss Fanny had always understood my excitement and given me a pat or a calming word or walked me up and down a little. But Mr. Roger had found a crony; he was sitting sideways on my saddle smoking a cigar and they were talking in loud voices about a dance they'd been to and discussing the merits of the various young ladies in a very disrespectful way.

I began to fidget and twirl about, forcing Roger to sit properly, for all the knowledgeable riders were slipping away. The Vicar came past on his stout white cob. 'Your sister's horse doesn't approve of your coffee housing, Roger,' he laughed, 'you'd better get moving.'

'He's had far too much of his own way,' said Roger jerking my mouth and kicking me with his spurs. I had stood all I was going to so I gave a plunge and a buck and shot off up the track. We were just in time. Hounds had found and were pouring out on the far side of the covert. The huntsman blew the 'goneaway' as he galloped on with the main body of the pack, the whippers-in were cheering on the tail hounds.

'Hold hard! Hold hard! Give them a chance,' shouted the master, as with one hand held up, he tried to control the eager riders. We horses were wild with excitement, the clamour of hound and horn had gone to our heads. The riders crammed down their hats and shortened their reins and then we were off, across a great grass field with a tall, dark bullfinch ahead. I leapt clearing the solid part of the hedge brushing through the straggling branches above, Mr. Roger protected his face with his arm, there was a yawning ditch, I stretched out to clear it and landed in the next field. Hounds were bearing left-handed, I went after them.

I could give you a fence by fence account of that hunt, but I know from my own experience at Earleigh Court, where tired hunters *would* describe in detail every leap they had taken during the day's sport, how very dull such accounts can be. But it was a long and fast run and Roger's weight and riding were a great hindrence to me. He seemed to think that great activity from him was needed at every fence and he would spur away at all the wrong moments. He held me on a tight rein when we went downhill, he sat on the back of the saddle belabouring me with his stout hunting crop when we went uphill. He liked to be masterful but he did none of the things a good master should: picking the good going, steering his horse away from rabbit warrens, choosing the easiest line of country as his horse tires, slowing him for a breather.

We seemed to gallop for miles without a check. I was labouring, rolling in my stride, my breath was coming in gasps. There were very few horses left with us, but I was determined to keep with hounds. I was giving all I had, but those spurs were still prodding my

sides, that crop still drumming on my ribs. There was a stile in a hairy hedge. I gathered all my remaining strength for it was uphill and both take-off and landing looked slippery. Instead of keeping me together and sitting very still Roger lurched in the saddle, brandished his whip, spurred me violently and shouted 'Hup'. I suppose he thought he was encouraging an unwilling horse to jump, but he disorganised everything. I slipped as I took off, landed awkwardly and felt a sharp pain shoot up my off fore leg, but I recovered my balance and galloped on struggling up the hill.

Mercifully hounds had stopped. They were milling round several holes beneath the windswept trees of a sandy knoll.

'Gone to ground, dammit,' grumbled Roger, as the huntsman blew the call. Other horses came struggling up the hill to join us. Their riders jumped off, turned their heads to the reviving wind and loosened their girths. Roger sat slumped on my back, a terrible dead weight. Sandwich cases, and flasks appeared.

As I cooled off I noticed the bitter chill of the wind and I was glad when the huntsman called hounds together and we set off downhill. There was no sign of the second horsemen. Several gentlemen said that their animals had had enough and they would go home, the rest of us jogged wearily to the next draw. I felt very tired and my off fore was still giving me twinges of sharp pain, so I felt no disappointment when we drew the covert blank. We hacked on to a larger covert and still the second horses had not come up.

This time we found and we were soon galloping

across open country, but I felt none of my usual fire, I was jumping carefully saving my off fore. Roger didn't notice that anything was wrong and I feel sure I was only saved from breaking down completely by a check, and the arrival of the second horse. It was a great relief to have Ben's light weight on my back and to set off for home.

For the first time in my life I failed to eat up and Ben and Mr. Johnson fussed over me offering gruels and mashes. Next morning they found that my foreleg had heat and swelling and I had to stand with water from the hose pipe trickling down it for an hour and then have linament rubbed in three times a day. It soon felt better, but for two days I was only led out for walking exercise up and down the drive. Then, on the third day I heard an angry voice outside my box, 'Well, is the wretched animal lame or isn't he?' demanded Mr. Roger. 'I've told you, Johnson, I'm not standing for molly-coddling that horse, he's got to take his turn with the rest. I need six horses tomorrow, for my two friends and myself. If we have Pegasus, Merlin and Jupiter for first horses that leaves Ebony, Sultan and Nimrod for the second string.'

'But you know Sir Clarence's views on hunting a horse two days a week, sir. He never permits it except in very exceptional circumstances,' objected Johnson. 'And two days with heat in a leg is asking for trouble; a strain can so easily become a sprain and then . . . '

'These *are* exceptional circumstances,' interrupted Mr. Roger. 'And I think it's a very poor business that with an establishment of this size I can't ask a couple of friends down without all this trouble over mounting them. In my opinion a stud groom doesn't know his job if he can't turn out six sound horses for a bye day.'

'Very well, sir,' said Mr. Johnson controlling his anger, 'but I wish it to be clearly understood that you have gone against my advice and that if anything happens to Ebony I am not responsible.'

'Of course you're not responsible. In my father's absence I am master here and I'll thank you to remember it.'

Ben redoubled his efforts with the linament and I felt quite myself again and almost inclined to agree that Mr. Johnson was mollycoddling me. So the six of us set off quite cheerfully for the meet.

We saw our stable companions move off to the first covert and then we joined the rest of the second horses and guided by the master's groom, who had a list of the draws, we hacked quietly in pursuit of the hunt.

We came up with them at about one-thirty and found our friends very much exhausted. Pegasus complained of an overreach, Jupiter of a badly bruised knee, while Merlin, who was getting on in years, just stood with his head drooping.

The three young men still seemed very full of spirits. They mounted us and were off larking over fences before hounds had found a fox. At first we entered into it all enthusiastically. Mr. Roger knowing of my ability to leap anything in cold blood, challenge his friends first to a brook and then to some park palings that were quite five feet. They were looking round for something else to jump when the master realised what was going on and called them to order. Then hounds found and we were off, our riders urging us on, putting us recklessly at the highest part of every fence and showing off to each other in a very wild manner.

As we grew tired the fun began to pall, but the young men seemed to have forgotten that we were flesh and blood. The run was a very long one, but if they had saved us at the start I think we would have finished, for we were all very fit. As it was, the larking about and racing had taken it out of us and we dropped farther and farther behind. Then poor Nimrod fell, crashing heavily into a ditch and lay there exhausted. He was pulled out, got back on his feet and remounted. We went on, following the tracks of the vanished field into the gathering dusk. Sultan stumbled twice and all but fell with exhaustion. My foreleg was giving me considerable pain and I was soon so lame that even Mr. Roger noticed. He swore and dismounted. 'Here's a fine thing,' he said, 'What a collection of old crocks! I'm going to advise my father to dismiss Johnson, the man's useless; then he can send this lot to the knackers and buy some decent horses.'

The friends had dismounted too. 'There's a small farm down there,' said one of them pointing. 'Shall we make for it?'

'Yes, there's nowhere better in sight. With luck the farmer will have some sort of trap and we can get home in that and leave the brutes here for the men to fetch.'

It was a long painful hobble down to the farm and we were all hitched up in the stable while the young men told the farm lad to look sharp and get the trap ready, for he could see to the horses when they had gone. They drove off laughing and then the lad did his best to make us comfortable.

It was a small, rough farm and there was only one old horse rug which he put on Sultan who was trembling uncontrollably, Nimrod and I had to make do with sacks. He brought us warm water and then oats and hay. The oats were musty but the hay was quite eatable. The worst of it was standing tied in a stall, for my leg was very painful and swelling rapidly, and I did not like to lie down. Then my sacks slipped off and I began to feel very cold, the huge cart horse headcollar was rubbing my nose and my leg grew worse and worse. I was a very sad and miserable horse shivering there in the dark and I don't think my two companions felt much better.

It was about two hours later that we heard the sound of the returning trap and then the voices of Mr. Johnson and Ben come to our rescue. We whinnied and they came hurrying in with rugs and lanterns and then they fetched hot water from the farm house and made us gruel.

Mr. Johnson was very upset when he saw my leg.

'Well he has done it now. No more hunting for you, Ebony, not this season and maybe never. Just look at that tendon! Oh the wicked waste of it, ruining a fine young horse!'

'Whatever will Miss Fanny say?' asked Ben dismally.

'It doesn't bear thinking about, but what can a servant do in such a family matter? Run and ask the farmer's wife to put the kettle on again; a hot fomentation will help to relieve the pain.'

CHAPTER FIVE

A new home

I stayed at that farm for several weeks. They made two of the stalls into a loose box and Ben came over every day to attend to me while the veterinary surgeon would come and shake his head over me several times a week. When I could walk without too much pain they led me home to Earleigh Court and there Sir Clarence came to see me. He seemed very angry as he stood looking down at my misshapen leg, but all he said was, 'Miss Fanny is heartbroken.' And, 'Well, we'll try a summer at grass and then see if he is fit for light work.'

So I was turned out, not with the other horses for Mr. Johnson said I would only be tearing about making myself worse, but with Ambrose the old donkey who pulled the mowing machine that mowed the great lawns around the house. We had a pleasant paddock at the back of the stables and only an iron paling separated it from the drive that led to the church. This meant that we had plenty to see and Sunday was a very sociable day. I enjoyed the bells and the singing and the sight of the people streaming up and down to church in their best clothes; some of them went three times on the same day. Most people walked because of the horses having their Sunday rest, but sometimes a carriage came. Best of all I liked the Sunday school children and I used to wait for them by the fence and most of them would stop for a pat and a talk.

Ambrose wasn't much of a talker, but I grew fond of him and he partly made up for the loss of Sambo. I used to miss him when he put on his boots and went off to mow the lawns.

It was autumn when Miss Fanny came to see me. She looked at my leg sadly and then she told Ben who'd come with her carrying the headcollar and the sieve of oats, that she was to be married and would live abroad for several years and, in the circumstances Sir Clarence had decided that I should be sold to a friend of the family. A gentleman who had had a serious hunting accident and needed a well-mannered hack; a lady's horse, narrow and not too tall to mount, for he was still rather crippled from a badly broken leg.

So I was taken up from grass and given light exercise. Mr. Arkwright, my new master lived in the north and was connected with the Sir Richard Arkwright who had invented the mechanical spinning machine, so Johnson told Ben. He was a colliery owner with a great coal mine. 'Not an old family like Sir Clarence's,' Johnson said, 'new rich, but educated and gentlemanlike. He was the owner of a fine stable of hunters before his accident.' They all thought it a good place for me.

Mr. Arkwright hadn't the time to come south to see me, so he bought me on Sir Clarence's recommendation and I had to travel north by train. It was terrible, especially the shunting. I could stand the noise and the steam and the whistles, but the shunting backwards and forwards and all those jolts and bangs would have unnerved me completely if they had not sent Ben to keep me company.

It was already dark when we arrived at the end of our train journey and left the station for a gas lit street. Ben explained that we were spending the night in the town and hacking on next day and that as the new Railway hotel had no stabling, being built for those travelling by train, we were booked at the old coaching inn, The Bell, in the High Street.

We were greeted by a very old ostler and led into a great gloomy rabbit warren of a stable. He insisted on helping Ben groom me and I've never heard such hissing. He told Ben that he ought to hiss louder for there was nothing like it to stop the dust from the horse's coat going down into your throat and lungs. There were only half a dozen horses stabled there that night, but he told us that they had room for sixty and that twenty or thirty years ago they would be full up nearly every night. 'Them were the days,' he said, 'you'd hear the horn, and there was the stage coach pulling up outside; out with the fresh team of horses, get to work on the dirty, tired ones. Then there'd be all the private carriages and the post horses and on market days you couldn't move for horses, there'd be traps and gigs left everywhere, blocking the roads and alleys. But it's all gone, the railway killed it all.'

'And what happened to all the folk that worked here?' asked Ben rugging me up.

'Lost their jobs, took to the roads most of them,

tramped off to find other work. The booking clerks were all right, the railways took them on, but the coachmen – they never got over it. They'd been someone you see, people were proud to know them, proud to sit up on the box with them. They were famous. So when it all went they had nothing. Took to drink most of them, drank themselves to death.'

I spent a comfortable night, my bed of straw was deep and my nearest companion a peaceful piebald mare called Magpie. Ben had been less well looked after and arrived scratching furiously and complaining that his bed was full of fleas. He turned me out very well, saying that I must make a good impression on my new master, and then we set out cheerfully on the last twelve miles of our journey.

Our road led over the moors, the air was very fresh and clear and hills covered in purple and brown heather stretched round us in all directions. Ben was still whistling away and I was still gazing around me fascinated by this new world when we reached a grey stone village and passing through we came to tall iron gates in a grey stone wall and turned up a drive. We passed the side of a fine stone house and turned into a very pleasant looking stable yard.

We were greeted warmly by the grooms, but Ben and I both had difficulty in understanding their Yorkshire accents. I was taken into a large loosebox and word was sent to Mr. Arkwright that I had come. He appeared in a few minutes limping badly and walking with a stick, he was a fairly tall, thin man and you could see that he had been seriously ill, from the pallor and the deep lines of his face.

My rug was whipped off and Ben had my headcollar on and stood me up while Mr. Arkwright and his head man discussed me. They seemed very pleased and Mr. Arkwright asked how I'd taken to the train and the inn.

'No trouble at all,' answered Ben. 'He's a clever horse, if you use him right and give him time and he understands what you want he'll always do it.'

'Well he's certainly a nice looking animal so if he's steady enough he'll be just the thing,' said Mr. Arkwright giving me a pat. 'I can't manage a horse that plays up with this crippled leg.'

'If you get on the right side of Eb he'll do anything for you,' said Ben and his voice choked. 'They say Miss Fanny cried her eyes out at parting with him and I for one shall hate to see the old fellow go.'

Then they all went away and presently a strange lad brought me a feed.

I felt very homesick for Earleigh Court and all my friends there and was quite dejected for a few days. Everyone at The Hall did their best for me and they seemed to have been told about Sambo for they brought me every shape and size and colour of cat. I nuzzled them all politely and got scratched and spat at several times for my pains, but in the end a small tabby did decide to stay in my stable, she was a good mouser, but hadn't much to say for herself; I never had another cat friend like Sambo.

Mr. Arkwright insisted on trying me first. Draper the head man begged him not to in case I was not as quiet as I was said to be, or had been upset by my journey. But Mr. Arkwright, who seemed quite an obstinate man, said that if he couldn't manage a nine-year-old with perfect manners and suitable for a lady, the sooner he was finished off the better.

I was led to the mounting block and Draper held me tightly, but of course I was used to Miss Fanny mounting from the block and once from a gate when she dropped her whip out hunting, so I sidled up as close as I could and stood like a rock to give Mr. Arkwright confidence. When we'd got him up we went for a stroll down the drive and then we tried a trot and Mr. Arkwright seemed well pleased.

'He is so narrow that he doesn't cause me the pain that the cob did,' he told Draper, 'and he moves so well there's no jolting.' He patted my neck. 'If it wasn't for the error of reading too much that is human into the animal mentality I'd say he sympathised with me having been a crock himself.' He dismounted gingerly. 'I'll ride him round about the place for a week and then over to Blackmarsh.'

The Hall had been built in a very beautiful spot with the moors on three sides of it and small farms with hilly green fields, enclosed by stone walls and inhabited by flocks of sheep on the other. With Mr. Arkwright riding me daily I soon learned to know the neighbourhood. In two directions the moor seemed to go on, wild and deserted, for ever, and we had many rides over it and round the farms. Then one day we took the third road over the moor. It led us across a very high, bleak stretch and brought us to the head of a valley and a very different scene. Columns of black smoke rose from the tall chimneys and great dark mills of the manufactories. Mr. Arkwright, who always talked to me a great deal when we were out together, let me stand and look in amazement from the great factories themselves to the railway sidings and the coal for factory engines, to the rows and rows of little blackened dwellings where the people lived, then he said. 'It's mucky and ugly, Ebony, but the source of the nation's wealth. You don't grow rich and powerful on agricultural products and a beautiful landscape.' Then he turned me suddenly and we cantered away.

By the end of the week everyone in the stable trusted me and there was no doubt that Mr. Arkwright's leg, health and whole appearance had greatly improved. It was generally agreed that he was now fit enough to ride to Blackmarsh Colliery, instead of using the carriage or the dog cart as he had since his partial recovery.

We took the same road as for the manufactories, passed the head of their valley and then came down into an equally despoiled area. A land of black pyramids, called slag heaps, of blackened grass and blackened trees and even a stream which ran with blackened water. The sharp arid smell of coal filled my nostrils blotting out all other smells. We went through the wide gates into the colliery. There was a group of grimy buildings and the pit head, a great wheel supported on heavy beams above the shaft that went down deep into the ground. A tall chimney gave forth smoke, a noisy engine gave forth steam. Stout cobs and heavy horses passed me pulling carts of coals. Great trucks brimming with coals stood on the tramways that led down to a railway siding. Men and boys with black faces hurried about their business and over all hung an atmosphere of gritty dust and the overpowering smell of coal.

A bent old man hobbled out and took my rein. 'It's

grand to see you on a horse again, sir,' he said, 'and a fine looking animal too.'

'Yes. His name is Ebony and he answers to it,' said Mr. Arkwright climbing carefully down from the saddle. 'Look after him, Matthew, he's worth his weight in gold.' Then he vanished into a building labelled 'office' and I was led into another with 'Pony Sick-Bay' written up over the door. This turned out to be a stable, with a comfortable loose-box already prepared for me, and a row of stalls in which were tied several little ponies.

They were exceptionally sturdy ponies and with their strong necks, broad chests and round quarters, they looked like tiny cart horses. Their manes were hogged, every hair of their tails was clipped off close to the bone and they were all stallions. When Matthew had rugged me up and gone away I looked into the stall next to me. A little old grey nodded sleepily. His legs, thick and filled, were bowed with hard work, his body was covered with old scars and his elbows capped with large unsightly callouses.

'What do you little fellows do?' I asked.

The grey raised his weary head. 'We are pit ponies. We work in the mine pulling the tubs of coal from the coal face, where the men cut it, to the cage which brings it to the surface. It's a hard life,' he sighed and lowered his weary head. The bay in the stall beyond was younger. He told me that his name was Pipkin and that he'd been brought to the surface some weeks before because a runaway coal tub had crashed into him, all but breaking a hind leg.

'They've patched me up,' he said cheerfully. 'I'm almost sound now so I shall be going down soon. I shan't come up again until I'm past work like Tammy, unless I have another accident.'

'You live down there night and day?' I asked.

'Yes, there are stables underground, not as comfortable as this one. There's never enough bedding and, as you can see, we all have capped elbows through lying on the bare floor. Tammy can remember the days when there was always an inch or two of water on the floor, but they've drained that away.'

'And is it quite dark?'

'Not when the men are there, they all carry their special safety lamps. A naked light can cause an explosion because of all the gases that abound in the atmosphere. When I was brought up the light seemed so bright it was almost unbearable, but they put me in the dark little stable next door and let me become accustomed to it gradually.'

'Why don't they bring you up for Sundays and holidays?' I asked.

'Because this is a deep mine and so the temperature down below is always very warm and humid and the ponies brought to the surface frequently lose condition or catch chills. Also some ponies are frightened by the movement of the cage and there are terrible accidents when they break loose in their panic and hurl themselves down the shaft to their death.'

'It's the hardness of the work that does us in,' said a tiny chestnut who was called The Giant. 'I'm only eleven hands but I'm expected to pull great tubs of coal for two shifts a day, five days a week. The men only work one shift and we're only supposed to do ten hours, but the good ponies are often taken out twice, which leaves four hours out of the twenty-four for eating, sleeping and resting. You work till you can scarcely stand, your legs go, your wind breaks, cough, cough, cough, day and night. Tammy has seen ponies die at their work, but nowadays they bring us up before we quite come to that, but I'm finished, I'll never be of any more use.' He sighed and we all stood feeling very sad as he gave his hacking cough. Then Georgie, a little skewbald, spoke up from farther down the stable. 'The food and water is dreadful. I can't touch it. There's coal dust in everything. I became quite ill after only a week or two, that's why I've been brought to the surface.'

'The food is not *so* bad here,' Pipkin told me. 'The horsekeeper is a good one, he keeps the feed bins tightly closed against the dust and he does his best to keep the water supply pure. I've known ponies come here from pits where the water tubs were so foul they stank and yet the ponies must either drink it or go without, and where, though they worked so hard, their feed was a few oats in chopped straw. Here we are well fed, with almost as many oats as we can eat. Our roads are kept in reasonable repair, so that they don't trap our feet, also the roofs, for if the wooden supports are broken they can catch and drag at our collars giving us terrible sores. There are rules about the heights of roofs and the size of pony that may be used when the seams of coal and, consequently, the tunnels are small, as they are here. I have been along tunnels too low for me, one has to crouch and crawl and it is very hard work to pull a load in that cramped position. That is why the tiny ponies like Giant are overworked, there are so many places where only they may go.'

Mr. Arkwright seems such a kind and humane man,' I said, 'and all the horses at The Hall are so well looked after. I don't understand how he can allow you to be treated in this way.'

'It is all to do with money,' answered Pipkin.

Tammy raised his head. 'When I first went down there were old ponies who remembered the days when little children pulled the tubs. They wore a sort of harness and crawled along the tunnels pulling, just like we do now. There were even smaller children of four and five years, who used to sit in the dark all day opening and shutting the trap doors as the tubs came through. Then a law was passed and no women and no children under ten years were to be allowed to work underground, so the ponies were sent down instead. I suppose the coals must be dragged by someone.'

Mr. Arkwright was soon in the habit of riding me over to the colliery on four or five days in the week. I enjoyed the ride even in the wintery weather with frost nails in my shoes or, on several occasions, half a pound of lard in each foot to stop the snow balling, and when I got there I enjoyed the company of the pit ponies. Then one day I arrived to hear anxious neighs and I found that Tammy and The Giant had gone and Pipkin and Georgie had been moved into the stalls nearest my box. They both looked very worried.

'What has happened?' I asked.

'They were taken away in a sort of cart,' said Georgie plunging in his stall. 'If I could break loose I would follow.'

'It was the knacker, I think,' Pipkin told me softly and sadly. 'The head horsekeeper and the vet came round yesterday. They examined Tammy and The Giant very thoroughly and I heard the vet say that their useful lives were over. Oh, Ebony, I'm afraid they've gone for dogs' and cats' meat, their skins for leather and their bones for glue.'

I know that it is better for an old horse to be shot or poleaxed rather than left out in a cold field to die slowly of disease, but it seemed so very sad that Tammy and The Giant had had so little pleasure in their lives.

CHAPTER SIX

Trouble at the pit

I had belonged to Mr. Arkwright for almost two years and he was growing so much stronger that he was talking of hunting again, but Mrs. Arkwright was said to be very much against it and there was a lot of talk in the stable about who would win.

Then we heard that there was unrest among the miners. It seemed that the price of coals had fallen suddenly and the owners were refusing to pay the men a wage that had been promised, so they had come out on strike. Mr. Arkwright often rode me over to Blackmarsh but there was no longer a busy, bustling scene. The great wheel was still, the engine silent and the railway trucks empty. The men and boys stood at the street corners without work or pleasure.

Some of the women would run after us as we trotted by calling on Mr. Arkwright to save their children from starving.

Some children died, it was said, and Mrs. Arkwright took to sending soup over to them in the wagonette. The men grew leaner and leaner and took their skin-and-bone dogs poaching for rabbits and other game in the woods and all the keepers stayed at home, rather than come to blows with starving miners.

It must have been after seven or eight weeks that things came to a head. Early one cold, foggy afternoon a message reached the house that there was trouble at the pit. One of the lads was immediately sent off to Bruddersford with a letter and told not to waste a minute on the way, I was saddled and taken round to the front door. Mrs. Arkwright was there begging her husband not to go but he said he must and was quickly in the saddle. 'Now Ebony,' he said, 'put your best foot forward. The men are planning to mob the manager's house and break up the pit head equipment and I must see if I can do any good by talking to them.'

I enjoyed the exhilaration of an unexpected gallop over the moors though I had to keep a sharp watch out for rocks and holes, for Mr. Arkwright seemed preoccupied with what lay ahead, rather than our present safety. We reached Blackmarsh in about half the usual time and found that the gas lamps had been lit and the pithead, the wheel, the chimney and all the buildings looked blacker than ever in the yellow light. The iron gates had been taken off their hinges and thrown down and there were large groups of men some arguing, some agreeing, everywhere.

Their voices grew angry when they saw Mr. Arkwright and they began to crowd us answering his quiet words with shouts, swearing and threatening gestures. I didn't like being in the centre of this sea of surging, angry men. I tried to back away for sticks and clubs were being brandished round my head, but Mr. Arkwright rode me forward calling upon them to disperse and go home and not to do anything that they would afterwards regret. It seemed to me that we were losing the battle of words and that at any moment we would be set upon and I would have an eye knocked out by one of the vicious-looking sticks. I carried my head as high as I could and tried not to flinch but I was very frightened of the united anger of the crowd.

Just as I decided that our last moment had come, for one man had grabbed my rein and they were pressed round so close that I could see no way to escape, except by plunging into them and trampling on the fallen bodies, there was a shout and a cheer and then a crash of breaking glass across at the manager's house. The crowd turned and then, as more crashes and more cheers followed, they ran to join this new sport.

A crowd of men and boys were pulling up the railings round the manager's garden.

'Where is the Mayor,' muttered Mr. Arkwright, 'what the devil's holding him up?' He took out his watch. Every pane of glass had vanished from the conservatory and the crowd were looking round for new victims. A man appeared suddenly with a flaming torch. 'Burn 'em out,' he shouted. 'Get some straw from the stable. Come on we'll burn the rats out.' Half the crowd cheered, but the other half shouted against it. One of the women called 'There's children in there,' but another shouted, 'they don't care if ours starve.'

A lot of people were calling to the man with the torch to put it out, but he made a sudden dash towards the front of the house and at the same moment Mr. Arkwright said 'Come on, Ebony!' and we shot forward too. The crowd had cleared from the front so we had a clear path and reached the man just as he was thrusting the firebrand through one of the broken panes. I stopped right against him and for a moment he and Mr. Arkwright wrestled for the torch, there was a smell of oil and smoke, sparks landed on me. Then Mr. Arkwright had it. I turned. The crowd was shouting and cheering again and some of the young

men were running up for an attempt to recapture the torch, everyone was pressing in on the side where the railings were down. The railings which still stood were a fair-sized jump, but I didn't mean to be trapped in the garden. I broke into a canter hoping Mr. Arkwright's leg was up to it; if he fell off . . . He was quick to realise my intention. He had the flaming torch in one hand but I felt him get the other hand down and grip my mane, I knew he was doubting his leg too. I took the railings as smoothly as I could, the landing was hard, but we were out on our own.

There was a roar, half annoyance and half admiration, from the crowd and then Mr. Arkwright was guiding me. He rode to a stone water trough, that was there for the benefit of the coal cart horses, and plunged the firebrand in; it hissed and died. I was thinking that the coal cart horses were not going to be pleased with the taste of oil, charred wood and cloth when there was a clatter of hoofs and a carriage came rattling through the colliery entrance.

'The Mayor at last,' said Mr. Arkwright who was binding a handkerchief round his hand.

The Mayor, who seemed to be a very ordinary man with a gold chain round his neck, climbed up on the box of his carriage and while his coachman held a light and two policemen stood guard below he read out something called the Riot Act. There was a lot about dispersing and departing peaceably to their habitations or to their lawful business and the more peaceful miners came to listen, but the less peaceful ones went on smashing up the manager's summer house and breaking the last of his windows. Then we heard the sound of many hoofs on the road and the special jingle soldiers make because of their swords and spurs. The shouting stopped, the crowd began to melt away. The soldiers stopped a little way down the road and one man fired his carbine into the air, the sharp crack made me start, but then they just walked in quietly and the officer came to talk to Mr. Arkwright and the Mayor. The horses were a smart-looking lot, strong but not fast, I decided. Mr. Wilson the manager had come out and joined in the conversation, it seemed that no one was hurt though his younger children had been much frightened. He and Mr. Arkwright began to make arrangements for the repair of the damage and some of the soldiers went to hoist the great iron gates back on their hinges. The Mayor left and at last Mr. Arkwright decided that we could go too.

It was very dark and there was no moon but we set off cheerfully for we knew the road well and the night is never so black when you have been out in it a little. We passed the valley of the manufactories and stopped for a moment to look down at the great cotton mills, every window blazing with gas light, smoke and steam and the red glow of furnaces all rising up from the valley and then being swallowed into the vast darkness of the sky.

As we climbed higher we found fog and the higher we went the thicker it grew, swirling round us, nuzzling us with its wet kiss, blotting out everything. Mr. Arkwright dismounted and led me. He was limping and I could see that the hand he'd hurt getting the torch was paining him. We were both cold and tired now that the excitement and terror of the evening had died away.

We plodded on wearily, following the road by the feel of its hard surface beneath our feet and noticing the change directly if we strayed on to the turf or heather at the side. Then we began to go downhill and the fog was thinning a little and suddenly I knew we were on the wrong road. I stopped and lifted my head and sniffed the air. Mr. Arkwright swore. 'We must have gone wrong at the crossroads on the top,' he said. 'I don't see how we did it, except that all senses of direction are suspended in a fog. Come on Ebony, we'll have to go back.' We turned and I began to hurry I'd had enough of this outing and wanted my supper and stable. Suddenly Mr. Arkwright slipped and fell. For a moment he rolled and twisted in pain, then he half sat up. 'This really is the last straw!' he said. 'I've done something to that ankle and they'll never find me here though they search all night.' He felt his leg gingerly and then he made an attempt to rise. I positioned myself near him thinking that he might like to pull himself up by the stirrup. He took the hint and got himself up on his good foot then he tried to put the other to the ground, but gasped and staggered and would have fallen had I not been there to lean against.

Carefully he lowered himself to the ground. 'I must stay here until I'm found. Well, the weather's not too bad. Many a man has died up here, lost in the snow, but I shall get away with an uncomfortable night and a chill. If only I was not so damnably cold already.' He looked at me. 'Go on, Ebony, home.' He clapped his hands and clicked his tongue. 'Go on, raise the alarm and, even if you can't tell them where I am, at least you'll be in a warm stable and there won't be two of us down with pneumonia.'

I felt very reluctant to leave him, but I set off, reins and stirrups dangling, at a purposeful walk. I went uphill back into the thickest fog and tried to find the homeward road. I was at the cross-roads and wandering uncertainly when I heard the sound of hoofs and the rattle of a trap. I neighed and hurried forward to meet it. Storm's neigh answered mine. I trotted down the road neighing with joy. It was the dogcart with its lamps lit and voices called, 'Mr. Arkwright, sir, are you all right?' Then they saw my empty saddle. 'Oh God, the Master's had another fall.' 'Jump down Harry and see if Ebony's all right,' directed Draper. 'Here take the lamp and look at his knees; has he been down?'

'No, not a scratch on him.'

'Well keep the lamp and walk on. Go carefully we don't want to injure him if he's lying senseless in the road.'

I had no such fear so I dragged Harry along at a brisk pace trying to show him that I knew what I was doing.

'Watch the sides of the road too,' called Draper. 'He may be lying on the grass and we don't want to miss him.'

We came to the cross roads and this time I was certain of my direction and when Harry tried to continue along the Blackmarsh road I refused to follow.

'Here, where do you think you're going, Ebony? It's this way,' he clicked at me and tried to pull me forward. From behind Draper flicked me with the driving whip, 'Come on,' he said. 'No messing about, we've got to find the Master.'

I pulled hard and dragged Harry down the right road, hampered by the lamp he could only pull me round in a circle, and when he tried to get me going again, I jibbed. Both men shouted at me. I still refused to move. They were getting angry, Harry jerked roughly at my mouth, I reared. Draper gave me a sharp cut with the whip. I reared again, higher. And as I came down, narrowly missing Harry with my hoofs, I twisted and plunged and wrenched the reins from his hands. I had galloped a few strides down the road before I trod on the reins flapping round my feet and jagged my mouth severely. They broke. I trotted a few more yards and turned to see if Harry was following me. He wasn't, so I neighed. He came on and I waited for him. Then, as he got near, I whirled away, he followed me cursing. I did this several times and then Draper began to call from the cross roads, 'Leave him, Harry come on back, we've got to find the Master.'

Harry wavered. I neighed loudly and then listened. There came on the foggy air a faint answering shout. Harry heard it too. He waved his lamp aloft and shouted, 'there's someone down here.' I moved on hoping that I was going to find Mr. Arkwright. Harry followed ignoring the distant shouts from the cross roads. Suddenly a voice said, 'Well done, Ebony, whom have you brought?'

'Is that you Mr. Arkwright?' asked Harry holding the lamp high, and then, suddenly seeing him. 'Oh thank God. We never thought to find you here. Are you much hurt?'

After that it all went easily. Harry ran back to tell Draper. There was a flask of brandy and a rug in the dog cart so Mr. Arkwright was soon feeling better and then they lifted him in. Harry made me reins of a piece of cord and mounted and we set off for home. The dog cart took the shortest way, but Harry and I went round by the doctor's house and asked him to come quickly to The Hall.

They made a great fuss of me in the stable that night. Harry gave everyone a very dramatic account of how I had reared and plunged and led him to the Master. Mrs. Draper came with a bowl of apples and carrots and brought all the little Drapers to admire me.

As for Mr. Arkwright it seemed that he had dislocated his ankle, but as it had never been quite right since his hunting accident, there was hope, that now it was properly put back by the surgeons, there would be an improvement.

He never tired of telling people that I had saved his life, or very nearly so, *and* the manager's house on the same day.

CHAPTER SEVEN

The explosion

Another year passed. Mr. Arkwright did manage a day or two's hunting, but we regarded ourselves as old crocks and came home early. The countryside was so wild that speed and jumping ability were far less necessary than in the south, but the pace was more suitable for a horse of my age.

Then spring came earlier than usual for the north and a long hot summer followed.

It was on a particularly hot and heavy day in August when I was standing in the Blackmarsh stable, I was dozing, undisturbed by the familiar sounds of steam engines, clanking trucks and passing coal carts. Then suddenly there was a strange trembling of the ground beneath our feet, followed by a muffled bang and then a much nearer crash. Then men's voices began to shout and alarm bells sounded.

Thoroughly awake, I listened. It was impossible to see what was going on, but it seemed to be to the pit head that everyone was running. Then Matthew came in to saddle me. He seemed very disturbed and kept shouting at the boy to bed down the spare stalls and fill all the pails with clean water and put the medicine chest ready. The boy was crying, 'My Dad's down there, and my two brothers.' 'And so are my sons and grandsons,' answered Matthew. 'Now, where's young Wilson?'

Young Wilson came, he was a youth, dressed for the office, but he soon scrambled up on me.

'Take it steady,' advised Matthew, letting go of my rein. We set off at a brisk trot and took the Bruddersford road as we turned out of the gate. He wasn't much of a rider but he had the sense to give me my head and he could click his tongue and cry 'whoa' so I understood him. We went into the town at a steady trot, there was no grass and the road was too hard for a canter.

Our first stop was the hospital, he hitched my reins over the railings and ran in. Then we went to the

police station where he told them of the explosion from the steps and then on to the telegraph office where I was hitched to some more railings and waited a very long time with flies buzzing round my head. By the time he came back the news had spread and the whole town seemed to be calling to us. 'How bad is it?' 'How many are missing?' 'Are there many trapped?'

And young Wilson called back that he didn't know, that the cage had been damaged in the explosion and so far no one had been brought up.

All the way back we passed groups of anxious-looking women hurrying towards Blackmarsh to ask for news of their menfolk. Many of them had several small children with them and some carried babies.

Young Wilson didn't leave me at the stable but rode me right up to the pit head. I had never been so close before and when I saw the shaft, black and bottomless beneath the shadow of the great headstocks and wheel, I began to snort nervously and back away. The men gathered round the shaft seemed to be shouting to men down below. Engineers struggled with cables, instructions were called from the engine house, people ran to and fro with messages and orders.

'Right, we're ready to try again,' shouted an authoritave voice. 'Stand back, stand back,' became the general cry, someone told young Wilson to 'take that horse away.' We moved back a little but stayed to watch. There was a good head of steam, the wheel was moving slowly. There was a murmur of relief from the watchers, the cage was coming up.

We waited fearfully to see what would emerge when the gates opened and it was a sad sight. Men staggered out supporting damaged hands and arms or holding bloody cloths to their heads or faces, some were carried out by their fellows others had to be laid on stretchers. Mr. Arkwright was there directing the long string of carts and wagons that had been collected to take the injured to hospital, and they were laid gently on the fresh straw and driven slowly away. The news was being passed from mouth to mouth, there were so many injured, so many missing, this man had seen his mates killed, that one had been parted from his in the dark and smoke and panic. A huge rockfall was reported here, a fire there. Mr. Arkwright was questioning some of the less seriously injured. Young Wilson managed to catch his attention for a moment and told him that the hospital were sending a doctor and a nurse to deal with the most badly hurt and had prepared all their beds; that the police were on their way and that he had telegraphed as ordered. 'Well done,' said Mr. Arkwright absently. 'Well, put that horse away, see he has a drink. You'll be needed in the office to help make up lists of the injured.'

A great many injured men were brought up before the first pony found its way into the cage, but presently three very frightened, trembling little animals were led into the stable. One was rather burned and singed, another had a severe cut and the third was unhurt. He said that there had been a great wind and then a terrible bang and flash, the air had rushed past him and there had been a dreadful rumbling and falling of rocks. 'My boy unhitched me from the tub,' he said, 'and we ran together.'

The pony who had taken such a singeing said that he had been near the East Stable, drawing a load of pit props and when the explosion came all the wood and hay in the stable caught fire. 'My boy unhitched me and we got away,' he said, 'but the ponies that were in the stable made a terrible noise, pawing and trampling, neighing and groaning; they couldn't get out.'

The cut pony told me that he had been hurt by a pony that took fright and bolted still harnessed to his tub and that there were many ponies down there too badly hurt to be worth bringing up. They all three stood trembling from their fright and the horrors they had seen and heard and I wondered if men really needed coal badly enough to risk all these lives.

Then more and more frightened and injured ponies began to arrive and the stable was soon packed out. There was a veterinary surgeon as well as several horsekeepers trying to deal with them and the unhurt ones were being bundled out into a nearby field. I was taken out and tied to a ring in a wall, for my stable was needed, so I stood watching the carts and wagons coming up from the town to take the rest of the injured to hospital. There were many women standing in silent misery, waiting for husbands and sons who had not been brought up, and there were many children crying. I watched all the ponies coming by, hoping to see my friend Pipkin, but I never did and I fear he may have died in the East Stable.

The offices seemed to have been given over to the doctor and nurse and those who were too badly injured to stand the jolting of the wagons, and Mr. Arkwright and Mr. Wilson and all the chief engineers were gathered round a table outside. The table was spread with maps and plans and they seemed to be arguing on a plan of action. In the end they seemed to decide on two plans, for Mr. Wilson, some of the engineers and a lot of men and equipment, were loaded on several wagons and drove away, the bystanders told each other that this party were going to try to reopen an old shaft on the far side of the rock fall. Meanwhile the other party, led by Mr. Arkwright, had equipped themselves with lamps and tools and were preparing to go down in the cage. They were going to try to bore a hole through the rockfall and reach the entombed men that way.

The wheel turned and the cage disappeared from our view. Everyone waited. The sad and anxious women, there seemed to be hundreds of them, were very quiet and resigned. Some of the children still cried, but only softly. In the stable a badly injured pony groaned. The flies buzzed round my head but the heat of the day had passed. There seemed to be no more to do above ground. I rested each leg in turn as I waited.

A boy brought me a bucket of water and a bundle of hay and some ladies appeared in wagonettes and governess carts and began to dispense food and drink to the waiting people. We ate and drank and went on waiting.

The shadows lengthened, the flies ceased to torment me and then, suddenly, I felt that strange trembling of the ground beneath my feet and again it was followed by a muffled bang, this time I knew what it meant, I did not need the wail that went up from the waiting crowd to tell me that something terrible had happened.

The cage still worked and there were still men prepared to go down to rescue their fellows, they vanished and we waited again, this time my heart was heavy and anxious too. At last the cage rose slowly to the surface, but only the second party of rescuers walked out. The others were laid on stretchers and each still form, covered by a blanket, was carried sadly to the office.

Then Matthew came with my saddle and bridle.

'You must take the bad news to The Hall, Ebony,' he said. 'It's a sad day's work. Mrs. Arkwright's only suffering the same as the other women, but his death will bring changes, changes for all of us.'

The news of the explosion, the many deaths and above all the loss of Mr. Arkwright, cast the deepest gloom over The Hall, but the plight of the entombed men and ponies made our own futures seem insignificant. We heard that the rescue attempts were continuing that an airway had been drilled, that tapping noises and faint hymn singing had been heard. And there were endless conversations about fire damp, about gases which exploded on meeting a spark or naked light, and gases which were called 'bad air' and killed as you breathed them in.

After three days the news came that thirty-nine men four ponies and a small dog had been got out alive and the rest of the missing were presumed dead. That was one hundred and seventy men and boys and I never heard how many ponies. Then the funerals took place. I didn't go but some of our carriage horses did, for though a great many black horses were hired for the occasion, with so many dead they could not get enough.

That ended the good days at The Hall. Mrs. Arkwright was taken ill and had to go away and Mr. Edgar Arkwright, the son who came to see to everything, had no liking for the north and said the whole place must be sold lock, stock and barrel. The grooms and the servants were all given their notice and we horses were sent down to the nearest large horse dealer to be sold.

CHAPTER EIGHT

Clarendon Mews

Mr. Edgar Arkwright hadn't bothered to find us good homes, but Draper and Harry who delivered us to the horse dealer's yard did their best for us. They gave us all very good characters and explained the sort of work for which we were each best suited. I was to be sold as a patent safety for a lady and the dealer said he did not think there would be any difficulty for, though I was getting on, I was in perfect condition and he knew my history.

He was right, I was sold on the first day. A very large man called Mr. Rawlings came with his dark and rather sullen groom, Hopkins. Mr. Rawlings announced in a loud voice that he wanted a reliable hunter for his daughters. Good-looking but not too pricey, while Hopkins peered at my teeth and felt my legs. Then Hopkins rode me, he was slightly better than young Wilson, but not much. Mr. Rawlings decided not to try me, for which I was very thankful for he looked quite twenty stone, but they put a side saddle on me and the dealer's little daughter rode me. She was really first rate so we put on quite a display and both enjoyed ourselves; I wished she could be my new owner.

Mr. Rawlings lived in a tall, town house fronting a wide, tree-lined street and the stables were in the mews at the back. Two long rows of stables and carriage houses, with grooms' quarters above, faced each other across a narrow cobbled road with an archway at either end and each house in the grand street owned a stable in the mews. Our building had four stalls and space for two vehicles, hay, straw and harness. It was rather cramped and dark and not what I had been used to, but I told myself that if there were other horses and if the young ladies were like Miss Fanny I would be perfectly happy there.

Hopkins had fetched me from the dealers and the moment we entered the mews he began to swear at a boy of about twelve, called Percy, who seemed to be his only assistant. It seemed that the carriage horses must be put in at once and as the harness was dirty it must be wiped over when it was on.

' 'Er Royal 'ighness wants to go shopping. Not a minute's peace in this ruddy place,' Hopkins grumbled, thumping on harness and slapping the poor carriage horses when they protested. 'Here Perce, take this rag and clean the worst off them traces. Oh Gawd! There's mud on the floor of the carriage, get the brush, Perce, or she'll be kicking up'. Percy flew about doing the work, the carriage horses wriggled uncomfortably beneath their dirty harness and Hopkins changed into a brown livery. Then they all left, looking quite smart on the outside.

Hopkins was right when he said that there was never a moment's peace in Clarendon Mews but it wasn't entirely his employer's fault.

Hopkins hated mucking out and he hated us when we lay down and got dirty. He was always swearing at us or Percy because we were not ready. We never went anywhere without a last minute panic, some piece of harness of saddlery would be found to be dirty, a rein would be broken, a stirrup leather unstitched. It was the same with our food, the corn was always running out, or the chaff wasn't cut or the hay hadn't been delivered.

All this constant noise and chaos made me nervous and irritable especially as I had so little exercise and spent day after day facing the blank wall of my stall. The young ladies did not come to see their new hunter, much less ride him and Hopkins' idea of exercise was a fifteen minute trot round the back streets with him winking and smiling at all the pretty girls.

To add to my discomfort my coat felt neglected and dirty. Out at grass a horse keeps healthy without grooming, but stabled and wearing a rug he must be groomed thoroughly every day and this just didn't happen.

Mr. Rawlings left everything to Hopkins, he never came into the stable the whole time I was there, I suppose he was busy with other things and had no interest in our welfare. Hopkins would go to the house every morning at five minutes to nine to get the orders for the day and if there was a change of plan the kitchen maid would be sent running round to tell us.

At last word came that Miss Helen and Miss Beatrice would be riding on alternate mornings and that Hopkins was to accompany them on one of the carriage horses. He was furious for now he would have two saddles and bridles to clean as well as the harness. He would be out riding in the morning and driving in the afternoon and, with the winter parties beginning, the carriage was often out at night as well. It was a lot for one man, but if he had taught Percy how to do things properly he could have been more use.

Miss Beatrice and Miss Helen were plump girls with round faces, round yes and round mouths that were always emitting little screams and shrieks, which was very unnerving to the horse that was carrying them. They didn't trouble to ride well and Hopkins was no teacher. They preferred to go round the town bowing and smiling to their friends rather than take the road which led out to the country.

I was filled with trepidation when I heard that Beatrice had decided to hunt me. Hopkins was sitting on a bucket reading the racing page, 'Go on, use some elbow grease,' he instructed Percy without looking up. ' " 'E's got to look a picture Hopkins", that's what she told me. Silly little madam. She's going man-hunting, not fox-hunting. Their Pa thinks they'll meet a better class of young man in the hunting field, that's what I 'eard 'im tell 'er royal 'ighness, so now Miss Beatrice is going to show off her charms to young Lord Beswick and the Hon. Walter Pym.'

'I can't reach his ears, honest I can't', wailed Percy.

'Well stand on the manger then.' I hastily lowered my head.

I felt ashamed of my appearance as Hopkins riding Sinbad led me to the meet. My coat was dirty and dull, my bridle was stiff, the twisted curb chain dug into my chin groove, and the saddle had been made for a much wider horse.

Mr. Rawlings had driven his family to the meet with Sailor in a borrowed wagonette and I felt even more ashamed as Miss Beatrice, with many little screams, was pushed up into the saddle. I never knew two girls with less spring and Hopkins used to say that it shortened his life by six months every time he legged them up. Once in the saddle Miss Beatrice paraded up and down bowing at everyone, ogling the younger gentlemen and giving little screams of apprehension if any of the other horses swung round or pranced.

At last we moved off. Miss Beatrice seemed inclined to ride near the front which pleased me for I had resolved to give her the hunt of her life and teach her what a pleasure it could be. She had manouevred us beside the Hon. Walter Pym and was giving little squeals of joy whenever he spoke to her. He sounded a very dull young man to me. He made a few remarks about the weather and laughed a very loud 'Ha, Ha!' after each one as though he had said something funny.

Young Lord Beswick seemed to have more sense and he even shushed Miss Beatrice when she gave squeal at covertside and told her that she must keep quiet, for she would distract the hounds or, worse still, head the fox.

Hounds found quickly. Some riders cut through the wood and others took the track round the outside. I followed this party for it is difficult to take ladies safely and quickly through trees, there is too much of them on one side. We galloped across a field, Miss Beatrice was already bumping about and out of breath. There was a small hedge and the Hon. Walter Pym called, 'Miss Rawlings, follow me.'

I followed his horse, but it ran out and half a dozen other riders cannoned into it. While they were all cursing each other, I circled and popped over. Miss Beatrice hung on by the reins which hurt my mouth and gave a small scream as her hat came off, but hounds were ahead and there was not time to stop for hats.

I gradually slipped into a really fast gallop, it was wonderful, just what I had been longing for. There was a small post and rails ahead, another hedge, then round the headland of a ploughed field through a gate and we came up with the hounds; they'd checked, the huntsman was casting them. I slowed up and joined the other horses; I was out of breath, but what could you expect with no exercise. Suddenly I became aware that all was not well with Miss Beatrice; loud sobs were coming from my back and several gentlemen were hurrying to her assistance. 'He bolted with me,' she sobbed, 'I pulled and pulled but he wouldn't stop. Oh, help me down. I won't ride another step.'

'I don't think he really bolted,' said young Lord Beswick helping her down. 'He looks a good sort of old hunter. I'd just sit tight and leave it to him.'

'Miss Rawlings finds that she cannot hold her horse,' he said handing my reins to Hopkins. 'I don't think the animal was to blame, she is not experienced enough for the hunting field,' and mounting thankfully, he galloped away.

We went drearily back to look for Miss Beatrice's hat and then turned for home. I was thoroughly depressed, Miss Beatrice was tearful because her hair had come down and she had mud on her face and Lord Beswick had galloped away and left her. And Hopkins was furious because there were three dirty horses, one set of harness, two saddles and bridles and a borrowed wagonette to be cleaned. He didn't do any of it properly. He left our stables dirty and slung our rugs on over mud and sweat and worst of all my bucket wasn't re-filled when I drank it dry so I spent the whole night longing for a drink of water.

I had another ignominious hunt. Two Saturdays later Miss Helen thought she might succeed where her sister had failed, but she didn't take any sensible steps beforehand. She didn't take me out for rides and get to know me, she didn't practise galloping and jumping, so I can only suppose that Hopkins was right and that it was young gentlemen she was chasing and not foxes.

This time it was a lawn meet so she probably enjoyed showing off her new habit in the house, but she took fright the moment she was put up on me, 'He's going to bolt, I *know* he is,' she cried and became so hysterical that Hopkins had to ride beside us with a hand on my rein. So there we were creeping along at the back with the little children on leading reins and the grooms on young horses. I was disgusted. Hounds found at once and we followed at a cautious trot. Then, even Hopkins' blood rose a little, and he permitted a sedate canter; gradually it grew a little faster. My eyes were on hounds, they had swung round in a lefthanded circle and were now only one field ahead. There was a tiny hedge, Sailor said that he could manage it so we strode towards it side by side. There was a scream from my back and then, as I took off,

Miss Helen flung herself from the saddle. The new habit caught on the pommel and there was a rending noise before she rolled free. I stopped and waited, wondering if she would remount. But she was screaming hysterically that I had bolted and suddenly I felt that I could stand no more. Throwing my responsibilities to the wind, I set off after the vanishing hunt.

I chose my own line and took the fences as I came to them. I was filled with the familiar feeling of exhilaration and happiness. The country was an easy one, the fences of moderate size, so I felt no need of a rider to partner me.

We had a wonderful run and when I came up, out of breath and steaming with heat, after the kill the riders all laughed at me and someone asked, 'Enjoyed yourself, old chap?'

We had finished in stone wall country, miles from town, and there was trouble about getting me home.

In the end a second horseman was found who agreed to go a couple of miles out of his way and drop me at Clarendon Mews.

Hopkins was not pleased to see me back. He hit me a sharp blow on the nose, the moment the other groom was out of sight, and used me very roughly as he wisped the worst of the mud off and rugged me up. There was no mash, but I was feeling defiant and not too tired, so I was able to enjoy my feed and hay.

As soon as Hopkins left us Sailor and Sinbad told me that there had been terrible trouble over the hunt. Miss Helen had cried, Mrs. Rawlings had stormed and then cried, Mr. Rawlings had been furiously angry and blamed Hopkins, I was to be sold.

CHAPTER NINE

I join a fair

I wasn't the clean and elegant horse when I left Clarendon Mews that I had been on arrival. In fact I was dirty and unfit, with a staring coat and a mane and tail that needed pulling, when Percy put an old rope halter on me and led me to the horse sale. Worst of all for an old horse I had no reputation left and not even a respectable stud groom to vouch for my character.

I was tied to a ring in the wall between a shivering and half-starved pony and a stout carthorse and a round paper with a number on it was stuck to my quarters. I turned as far as my rope would allow me and watched the scene. There was a great many people, mostly farmers and tradesmen, but also some very rough-looking men and boys who swore and spat a good deal.

The noise was very great. The sellers were telling everyone what good animals they were offering. The frightened horses were all whinneying and there was an endless clattering of hoofs and cracking of whips as they were run up to show their paces to likely buyers. There were a few men already drunk, though it was not yet twelve, and they were shouting and singing.

It was very unpleasant having my mouth forced open by complete strangers who wanted to see my teeth. Some of them felt my legs, slapped my flank and pulled out my tail as well, before making a disparaging remark about my age and walking on.

The farmers all thought me too well-bred. 'You got to cosset that sort,' they said, or, 'I 'aven't the time to look after a blood 'orse.' The tradesmen all asked if I was broken to harness and Percy, who didn't know any better, said no, I was a hunter. The occasional person looking for a cheap hunter was always horrified by my age. The cart horse next to me was having a better time. The farmers all said that 'he was a likely sort'. He told me that he'd been working on the canals, towing barges, he enjoyed the life but more and more goods were going by rail instead of by water so he and many more like him, were out of a job. But, he added placidly, that he would be quite happy to work on a farm.

At last two men came who didn't dismiss me as useless. The younger was tall and thin with an eager, handsome face, the other short and fat, wearing rather old fashioned clothes and smoking a cigar. The young one, Felix, stood back studying me carefully and then said, 'I think we've found him, Alf. He's got presence, look at him, and breeding. Trimmed up a bit, well-groomed, he'd be exactly right; stupendous!'

'Except that he's not a mare,' said Alf. He looked at my teeth, 'Past his second youth. Is he sound? That's the question. And can he jump?'

'Oh yes, he can jump all right,' said Percy coming forward and he told them about my riderless hunt.

Felix laughed a lot. 'There, that clinches it,' he said. 'I knew at once he was the horse for us. Personality, looks quiet, friendly; a great jumper and any amount of character.'

Alf seemed less certain. 'We'll see what he fetches; I'm not paying much for a horse of his age. Here, boy, trot him out and let's see how he moves.'

I liked the look of Felix, I felt that he would be a considerate master and all that talk of jumping was music to my ears, but I hoped that he didn't want to hunt me in a fast country for I knew that I wasn't up to that sort of work any more.

Presently my turn to be sold came. I was walked and then trotted up and down amid a sea of white faces and brandishing whips, while the auctioneer called for bids. There was no great eagerness to buy me. A few of the people who'd looked at me bidded, one sounded like the undertaker, another voice could have belonged to the cats' meat man, the third was obviously a farmer. Then I saw Alf waving his catalogue in a lordly manner. At last the auctioneer's hammer fell and I was led away and tied up. The half starved pony was being sold, I hoped he would go to someone who would give him a square meal, and not for cat's meat. Then Felix came up carrying a saddle and bridle. 'We got you for a song, old horse,' he told me. 'Now, where's that boy? I want to know your name.' Percy seemed pleased that Felix was to have me. He put on the saddle, while Felix adjusted the bridle to fit my head, then he sobbed a tear or two as he stroked my neck, but Felix gave him sixpence and told him I should have a good home.

As Felix mounted and rode out of the sale yard I knew that he was a good rider. He felt confident and easy, he didn't attempt to impose his will on me, but just rode me quietly forward while he learned what I was like. In no time we were partners, it was as though I had Fanny or Ned back again and my heart rose as we left the town.

It was a frosty day but the sun was high and warm and had already thawed most of the bone from the ground. Felix sang as we walked and trotted along and altogether he seemed very pleased and cheerful.

We passed through several villages and then we cantered over a short stretch of moor and came to a long lane, between stone walls, that brought us down to a grey stone farm in the valley.

It was rather a tumble down place and the yard instead of being full of pigs or cattle, had a whole collection of living vans within its walls, like gipsy vans they had little chimneys, two windows and shafts for the horse, but the people who came, to greet us weren't gipsies, though there may have been one or two among them. There were a great many children playing everywhere and a smell of paint and cooking filled the air.

Felix led me into a stable. I saw with pleasure that it was quite a large loosebox and when I looked over the low partition into the next box I found the smallest pony I had ever seen. He was skewbald and much smaller than The Giant. He could not have been more than eight hands. He said at once that his name was Tom Thumb, that he was the smallest pony in the world and came from the Shetland Isles. Felix was rubbing me down, someone was spreading my straw, someone else brought a bucket of water and yet another came running with a rug so I was soon very comfortably settled. When the humans had gone away and I had eaten my feed, Tom Thumb asked me what I did. I answered that I was a hunter and he didn't seem to find that at all satisfactory.

'I wonder what you'll do here, then,' he said. 'Oh well I suppose they'll teach you something. I jump through hoops, lie down, take handkerchiefs from my master's pocket, chase a boy round the ring and do numerous other tricks. I'm billed as The Clever Pony as well as The Smallest Horse in the World; people pay good money to watch me.'

I felt rather alarmed at this, but Tom Thumb, who seemed very pleased to have a companion, talked on and on. It seemed that he and his master Andrew had belonged to a circus, but there had been a fire and the equipment had all been lost so now they had joined this fair and soon we would all be travelling round the countryside performing.

I asked if he knew what Felix did and he answered that he was an actor and that sometimes a whole company of them went round with a fair, but he thought that Felix was the only one and he had been talking about an equestrian act. Then I asked about Alf and Tom Thumb said he was the Guv'ner and usually called 'His Nibs'. He settled the quarrels and arranged the fairgrounds and lent everyone money.

Felix seemed a very thoughtful master. The very next morning he spent a long time sawing and hammering at my door and when he had finished it was in two halves and the top one fastened back and enabled me to look out and see all the activities in the farmyard. I can't describe the pleasure that gave me. Being tied up in a stall is all very well for a short time and it's not so bad for a horse that is out all day doing slow work and only in his stall at night. But when a hunter or hack is condemned to spend twenty-two out of twenty-four hours, six or seven days a week, facing the same blank wall, well, it's no wonder that horses are driven to crib biting, windsucking and other nervous disorders.

After the boredom of the mews I was delighted with my view and made Tom Thumb so jealous with my accounts of all I could see that he began to work on the bolt of the door between our boxes. He got the head up and then slid it back with his teeth and pushing the door open and came in with me. Of course he wasn't tall enough to see over the door and he had to balance with one toe on the cross bar. When Felix found our two heads looking out he laughed and fetched a stout box for Tom Thumb's forefeet.

For a few days Felix just took me for rides in the country side. We jumped some walls and hurdles and a gate and he seemed very pleased with me and always told everyone that I was 'just the thing'.

Then one day he took me into the barn. The floor was scattered with peat and a ring was marked out in the middle, it was rather a small space, but I was well enough balanced to canter round it quite fast, which pleased Felix. We practised entering at a wild gallop and stopping dead in the centre. He was very careful of my mouth and threw his weight back as a signal instead of pulling on the reins and, as soon as I understood what he wanted, I did it all on my own. Then we started work on the whole act. After the gallop in Felix would make a speech all about his wonderful mare Black Bess and then another man called King would come in on one of the caravan horses and he and Felix, who was Dick Turpin, plotted together.

Then a very old coach came in, drawn by four very hairy horses and it was robbed by Turpin and King, several people fell dead and everyone fired pistols which made us horses jump at first though we soon became used to it. After that the police came and they captured King, and he called to Turpin to shoot the men who held him, but Turpin missed and killed King by mistake.

Then a great chase began. I would go round and round the ring at a gallop, rush out and come in again from the other side and the pursuers were doing the same though they never caught up with us. We robbed another coach; it was the same one really, but they put a different name on the doors and dressed the people differently, and there was some more firing of pistols.

The next exciting part was when a toll gate was put up in the ring. As Turpin and I came galloping in the keeper shut it to stop us, but Felix would give a shout and I would soar over. After that I had to show signs of tiring and when I could only proceed at a weary trot with my head low we stopped at an Inn and I was given a drench of brandy or ale or something from a bottle, only the bottle was always empty.

Then we came to the city of York and a large cardboard spire was put up and bells began to ring. I was reduced to a walk and Felix dismounted and led me and then it seemed I was supposed to fall down dead. This wasn't easy to learn. Tom Thumb could do it and I was made to watch him, but I found all his advice very irritating and really got on better when Felix taught me alone.

He would take me to a nice soft spot and strap up one of my forelegs, then he would tap my other knee with a whip until I bent it and kneeled down. The moment I did it I was praised and given oats or carrots. Gradually I learned to kneel without the strap and whenever he pointed at my knees. All he had to do then was to turn my head towards him and gently push my shoulder until I gave way and lay down on my side. I wouldn't have done it for Hopkins, but Felix was kind to me and made all my lessons enjoyable, so I decided to oblige.

I soon knew the routine and when we reached York and the bells began to ring, I would watch for the signal. When I had died Felix would make a long speech over my dead body and then the pursuers would come up and there was another fight. The first time this happened I raised my head to see what was going on, but this caused a great outcry from the watching children and Felix came and told me I had to stay dead.

The next problem was carrying me out. A great yard door was brought in and slid under as six strong men lifted me, then about twelve of them carried me out. I always hated this part but Felix would walk by my head and stroke my neck to keep me calm, so I put up with it.

CHAPTER TEN

Life as Black Bess

Though there were stablehands among the fair people Felix looked after me himself and by the start of the season I was a picture. Too round and well-covered to be hunting fit I was just right for a public performance, my coat shone, my mane and tail, neatly trimmed, were beautifully brushed out and this was just as well, for there were some very extravagent tributes to Black Bess's beauty in the verses Felix had to say.

On the day we moved out of our winter quarters all the carts and wagons and vans left very early in the morning. Felix and I started much later for we could take a short cut across country instead of going by the roads.

When we reached the fairground which was just outside a large town, Felix rode me to a tent with a large notice about Tom Thumb the Clever Pony and another saying that Captain Felix Fanshawe, late Royal Hussars, would present the stupendous equestrian drama *Dick Turpin's ride to York* with many spectacular fights and a thrilling performance by his famous horse Black Bess.

Inside was our usual ring and the cardboard Inn and spire and the toll gate and a couple more jumps were all ready at the side. I began to feel nervous but Felix rode me round until I was used to the tent and the lights and then he took me out to see the fair-ground. There were stalls for Hoop-la and ranges for shooting and coconut shies. There was a huge round-about with brightly coloured and richly gilded horses and a steam engine to work it. There were many little booths with fortune tellers and fireproof ladies and fat ladies inside. There was Professor Lopescu's Flea Circus from Rumania and a Punch and Judy Show and many slides and swings and entertainments of all sort.

As it grew darker more and more lights came on and the steam engines sent sparks and smoke up into the dark sky. There was a smell of burning coal and hot engines. Then a great steam organ started up. It was painted in bright colours and gilded like the horses and the noise from it was tremendous, as though a whole brass band was playing close at hand. I stood looking at the scene, turning this way and that to take it all in and Felix sat on my back laughing at my amazement.

When we went to the stable tent that I was to share with Tom he was being got ready for his act. He wore a silver and orange bridle, roller and crupper and from his forelock rose a very handsome orange plume. I wondered if I had to dress up, but no, it was Felix who came disguised. He had a curly moustache, a green coat and cocked hat, a belt full of pistols. Andrew was impossible to recognise with his face covered in white, a huge mouth and a false nose, he was dressed as a clown, and the small fat boy Tom had to chase had been made to look fatter than ever by very tight clothes.

When Tom left for the ring one of the stable hands put the finishing touches to my appearance, then Felix stopped brushing his coat and mounted and we walked over to the ring tent and waited in a dark corner.

Tom was pretending to become angrier and angrier with the fat boy and finally he chased him round the ring and out in a very ferocious manner. His Nibs, wearing black trousers, a scarlet coat and a top hat announced Dick Turpin, and Felix took me well back so that we could get up speed for our entrance.

We whirled in and round and came to a very dashing halt in the centre. Felix took off his hat and bowed low, I stared at the lights and the white faces all round me. Then Felix began the verses on how much he loved his bonny Black Bess. As he came to the last verse:

'*Mark that skin, sleek as velvet and dusky at night,*
With its jet undisfigured by one spot of white;
That throat branched with veins, prompt to charge or caress.
Now, is she not beautiful? Bonny Black Bess!'

King came riding in and they began to plan robberies.

We held up the coach, the horses were all looking a good deal smarter than they had at rehearsal and the guard had a horn to blow. There were the usual shootings and several deaths and then we made off with some bags labelled MONEY. King had taken too

many and could not control his horse, which was why the police got him.

When Felix's shot killed him all the audience groaned in horror but they cheered up when we took one of the extra jumps and galloped away. These brush fences were not very big but though I was supposed to leap over perfectly the pursuers, especially the police were meant to run into each other, fall off and generally make a hash of things and this pleased the audience very much.

Then we robbed the second coach and came to the toll gate. It had grown larger at every practise and was now a big jump, about five feet. I took it carefully for the lights were casting strange shadows and made finding the right take off difficult. The people cheered and clapped as I soared over. We stopped at the Inn and Felix had another long verse to say which ended:

'By moonlight, in darkness, by night or by day,
Her headlong career there is nothing can stay.
She cares not for distance, she knows not distress,
Can you show me the courser to match with Black Bess?'

Then I began to slow down and hang my head; soon I was only walking and then as the spire was put up and the bells began to ring, Felix led me. Right in the middle of the ring he pointed at my knees and I fell dead. The audience were very upset; I think some of them thought I really had died. Turpin was very upset too:

'Art thou gone, Bess? Gone – gone!' he cried out very dramatically. 'And I have killed the best steed that was ever crossed.

'O'er highway and byeway, in rough or smooth weather,
Some thousands of miles have we journeyed together;
Our couch the same straw, our meals the same mess;
No couple more constant than I and Black Bess.'

They fought the last fight and I managed to lie still and not look though it was very hard. Then the door came and they called for volunteers from the audience to help carry out poor dead Bess and I'm certain a great many people went home wondering whether I was really dead or not.

All the fair people thought the performance a great success and Felix kept patting me and saying 'Old horse, you're a natural, a born actor; stupendous!'

After that he became even more ambitious and besides adding new touches to our present act he was always thinking of other acts we could perform in the future and talking about *The Taylor of Brentford* and *The High-Mettled Racer* or, *The Fat Farmer*, who wore layers and layers of clothes and undressed as he galloped round the ring.

We seemed to be doing well. We moved from place to place sometimes only staying for one day and night, sometimes for five. By the summer we had reached the west country and I was jumping the toll keeper as he ran to bar the way, as well as the gate, we were practising for the *Taylor of Brentford* which called for a lot of acting on my part as I had to push Felix around and make disagreable faces and pretend to bite him.

In some places our audiences were so large that we had to do Dick Turpin three times over every evening. I did get very bored at having to go through it so often and we had to think of new things to do to keep up our interest, Felix invented that I should raise my head and give my thoughtless master a kiss with my lips before I died; this upset the audiences very much.

In the autumn we came near to London and the idea was that we would work our way north and back to winter quarters, except for those who had special Christmas engagements.

Then one night some men came round to the stable when the performance was over. The stablehand was rubbing me down and Felix was unsticking his moustache. They introduced themselves and asked him out to supper. He seemed very excited and changing quickly he went off with them leaving me to the stablehand.

Next day Felix seemed very thoughtful and he had a long talk with His Nibs. Our show went on as usual but we gave up rehearsing *The Taylor's Ride*. I sensed that something was wrong and I lost some of my enthusiasm. But he didn't say anything until one morning when we had just come to a new town. Then he came rushing into my tent; he was dressed very smartly in his best suit. He put his arms round my neck and said, 'I'm sorry, Ebony, I feel a brute, a complete cad doing this to you. You've been magnificent, you did everything you could to make the show a success, you never let me down once and now I'm walking out on you. But you see, old horse, it's the chance of a lifetime, you *can't* refuse a part like this. You just can't!

'If I had the ready cash I'd buy you from His Nibs and take you with me, but I haven't and no stable to put you in either. I'm truly sorry old horse.' He gave me a carrot and ran out of my stable. I couldn't believe that our happy times together had ended as suddenly and finally as this. For a day or two I thought he might come back, I would look for him in the mornings and when the time for our performance came, I felt sure that he would come bursting in, sticking on his moustache and telling me some new plan. Sometimes I thought I heard his voice and would whinny excitedly, but he never came.

Then I learned, from the talk of the stablehands,

that he had been offered a good part at a big London theatre and might well become rich and famous. For a time I clung to the idea that His Nibs was finding another Dick Turpin to ride me and things would go on much as before, but men appeared who looked at my teeth and felt my legs and had me trotted up so I knew I was to be sold.

'Too old for a hunter,' they all said, and 'who wants a circus horse, he'll be doing tricks in the road.' And they haggled with His Nibs over the price.

At last a man with very fair hair came, he said that he owned a large riding school and livery stable in London and needed a reliable, well-mannered horse for his lady clients and was willing to pay a good price for the right animal. So I changed hands again and now belonged to Mr. Chandler.

CHAPTER ELEVEN

A popular horse

I was amazed by London. One of our stablehands took me to an inn called The Three Horseshoes and there I was met by one of Mr. Chandler's lads, looking very respectable in proper groom's clothes, and he rode me into London.

The height and variety and extent of the buildings and streets amazed me, but the number of horses did so even more. There were pairs of horses pulling omnibuses packed with people, there were single horses in smart hansom cabs thin broken-down-looking horses pulling the four wheeled growlers, coal carts in their hundreds. Brewery drays drawn by three great Shires or Clydesdales. Railway van horses, Mail van horses, teams of horses pulling enormous loads from the docks.

We passed through a poor area where donkeys abounded, carrying every sort of goods in their little carts. We saw sweep's ponies, baker's ponies and butcher's ponies; horses drawing rubbish carts and water carts for laying the dust in the streets, and enormous vans full of the furniture of people moving house.

As we came deeper into London the carriages became more elegant. We saw beautiful horses, perfectly matched pairs, drawing exquisitely painted and polished carriages, with very smartly turned-out coachmen and grooms, in special liveries, on the box. Workman-like carriages and broughams taking the professional men, the lawyers and fashionable doctors about their business and all mixed up with them and crushed together in the street were the pony and donkey carts, the great drays and vans and the omnibuses.

The noise of wheels and hoofs, the shouts of the drivers the crush and the whole scene bewildered me and I was very pleased when I saw trees, a stretch of water and the green of a great park and then we turned down a quiet street and through a pillared gateway into a yard. The groom dismounted and led me up a ramp, it was a wide affair like a road, with a wall on either side and brought me into a great stable on the first floor of a huge building.

It was very light and airy with a high, partly glass, roof and there seemed to be seventy or eighty stalls; most of them were empty, but headcollars and folded rugs, hayracks and water buckets told me that they were only waiting for their occupant's return. There seemed to be some trouble about finding a place for me but eventually I found myself tied up with an empty stall on one side and a large black horse lying comfortably on a good bed of straw on the other.

'I'm tired out,' he said. 'Four funerals yesterday so they've given me a day off. Why all the people die the same week beats me. They say it's the influenza carrying them off. I wish it would carry them somewhere they don't need black horses. And it beats me why they put all those cemeteries on the tops of hills. Highgate, Finchley, Norwood, whoever fixed that wasn't thinking of horses, those carriages are blessed heavy to drag uphill.'

When he heard that I was new to London, Cardinal began to give me information. He said there were three hundred thousand horses in London and if you put them in single file they would stretch from St. Paul's to John O' Groats at the very end of Scotland, or so he had been told. But he knew for a fact that ten thousand horses worked on the omnibuses because an omnibus horse had told him. Their life was a hard one, he said, for all the starting and stopping was a great strain, and they only lasted for five years. 'But take the tram horse, he's done in after four years, and a doctor's horse only lasts six, all that waiting about in the wet and cold, you see, and night jobs.'

I was beginning to wonder how long I would last when six pairs of beautiful grey horses with white decorations on their bridles were led out.

'They're off to a wedding,' said Cardinal. 'People like greys for weddings and if they can't get them they take chestnuts.'

In the evening the horses who had been hired out for the day began to come back. At first it was a trickle and then a flood and I had never seen men work so hard and fast as those grooms cleaning the London dirt from them.

My companion on the other side was a strong active looking horse. He said he was a Cleveland Bay, but that he hadn't been bred in Yorkshire, and that his name was Trooper. He explained that he was kept in reserve, ready to go at a moment's notice when any horse hired out by Chandler and Barlow fell ill or lame. He explained that some people didn't like to be bothered with choosing horses or with keeping the number that were necessary if they were never to be inconvenienced by colic and lameness and chills, so they just hired what they needed from the job-master, and he undertook to provide a substitute at any hour of the night or day.

'Where I went today the lady had her own stables and groom, but a pair of Chandler and Barlow carriage horses. When one horse started ringbone she couldn't get out without her carriage, ladies can't go in hansom cabs alone, you see, so the cob boy took me over. I was the right colour but not showy enough to please, so she'll have another horse tomorrow.' He ate a few mouthfuls of hay and then told me that he was trained as a fire horse. Chandler and Barlow provided the horses for three fire engines and they had to keep replacements for them always ready. 'They telephone from the fire station and you have to get round there in a flash,' Trooper explained, 'but I'm not a regular fire horse, they prefer greys. They reckon the street clears quicker for a grey.'

I asked Trooper if it was dangerous pulling a fire engine and whether horses were often burned.

'There are a lot of accidents to horses,' he answered, 'but they happen most frequently on the way to the fire, galloping through all the traffic or slipping on the road. Of course the horses have to be trained to remain steady in the midst of heat and smoke, to stand the sparks raining down on them and not to mind the steam pump's engine for that is almost as terrifying to the green horse as the fire itself.'

The next day, after a good grooming, a very neatly turned-out groom mounted me. Two chestnuts, both wearing side-saddles, were brought out and the reins handed to him. So, with a horse on either side of me, I walked through some quiet streets to a large and elegant house.

Here we were evidently expected for a manservant opened the door and said that the young ladies would be out in a moment. Presently they came, very smart in black habits and curly brimmed bowlers. The groom put them up and then we set off for the park. The young ladies rode side by side chattering to each other and the groom and I followed a respectful pace or two behind. They were experienced riders so no demands were made on us and I was able to look about me.

The main streets were very dirty. I suppose with that great crowd of horses passing so constantly it was impossible to keep them clean, but they smelled like a farmyard and where the people on foot crossed the road to the park, a bent old man in a long ragged coat, constantly swept a way clean for them.

The park was very pleasant. There were huge trees and wide stretches of green, and soft peaty rides had been made for the horses. There were roads too for the magnificent carriages. We saw an open laundau drawn by a pair of high-stepping horses, a park phaeton driven by a lady with a pair of cream ponies and a tiny groom called a tiger sitting on a little seat behind. All the ridden horses were good-looking and well turned-out and the elegantly dressed riders were all bowing and smiling and sometimes stopping to chat with each other. We went all round the park and had a very pleasant canter or two and then took the young ladies home. I enjoyed it all very much.

When we were back in the stable Mr. Chandler came over and asked, 'How did the new one, Ebony, go?'

'Very well indeed, sir,' answered my rider. 'A perfect park hack, I'd say.'

'Did he shy at all?'

'Not once. No trouble at all and a beautiful collected canter.'

'Sounds all right,' said Mr. Chandler, 'but you'd better take him out once more.'

That afternoon I escorted the three Miss Fostergills, who had brown habits and bowlers, and the next morning I was tried out in the school. It was rather a small school, but my training for Dick Turpin's Ride had made me very well-balanced and Mr. Chandler soon saw that I could canter and jump without difficulty.

I gave several lessons that day and became heartily tired of that school.

I soon found that being a perfect park hack and a good school horse were great disadvantages in life. All the young ladies wanted to ride me and a good many, supported by their mammas, insisted on having me. Mr. Chandler found it very difficult to say No, partly because he was afraid of losing good custom and partly because he was a good-natured man, who did not like to disappoint any one. The consequence was that I became hopelessly overworked.

All that winter I would go out on the morning ride, the fashionable mid-morning ride and the afternoon ride and give lessons in the school as well. And if the weather was bad, if one of the thick London fogs came down or the morning was frosty I would just work hour after hour in the school instead.

A covered school with its soft going is certainly very kind to a horse's legs, but the boredom of staying within its walls and seeing nothing of the outside world, is very great. Especially when the work itself is monotonous and the horse is learning nothing new.

The young ladies all demanding their favourite, 'their dear Ebony', didn't realise what they were doing and Mr. Chandler didn't seem to notice that I had lost all interest and merely plodded round praying for the lesson to end.

I suppose I would have stood up to the work better if I had been in my prime of life, but I was an old horse and I soon began to feel and look like one. I missed Felix and all the change and excitement of our wandering life and I had no one to be fond of, the grooms and strappers changed constantly and had little interest in us horses. I lost all my old pride and became lifeless and at last one of the mammas noticed it, and asked for her daughter to be mounted on something more lively. 'A horse with a little more spirit'.

Mr. Chandler ordered me tonic powders in my food and with less competition to ride me I suppose things would have gradually righted themselves, if it had not been for the hoop.

There was a great fashion that spring for hoops. All the children in the parks and streets trundled them along. The boys had iron hoops and a sort of hook to guide them, the girls had wooden hoops, which they bowled with short sticks.

We had been for a ride in the park, where all was fresh and green. The chestnut trees were out, every house seemed to have window boxes full of flowers and the sun shone. But I had lost my pleasure in it all and just plodded along carrying one of my endless young ladies; I had long ago given up trying to tell them apart. We were walking home along a quiet street when a hoop suddenly shot between my forelegs. If I'd been strong and alert I am sure I could have avoided it, but stumbling along weak and half asleep, with my head low, I was in no position to take sudden action and as it entangled itself with my legs I slipped and fell.

Luckily I fell on my off side so I did not trap the young lady's legs under me and the groom jumped off and soon freed her from the pummels. I lay for a little feeling very sorry for myself. My forelegs were hurting and I was in no hurry to find out just how injured they were.

But a crowd was collecting. The little girl who had bowled the hoop was sobbing and her governess was scolding and several passers by were advising that the knackers cart or the vet should be sent for, so I struggled up. My near knee was gashed and a trickle of blood ran down my cannon bone, but it was the old injury in my off fore that pained me most.

Mr. Chandler was very put out. 'I daresay it wasn't the horse's fault but accidents of any sort give us a bad name. And supposing that cut leaves a scar? No one wants to see a daughter mounted on a horse with weak forelegs; on an animal that's been down.'

By next morning both my legs were so swelled that I could scarcely hobble a step and when Mr. Chandler came to see me he brought Mr. Barlow.

Mr. Chandler patted me but he seemed to be very unhappy about my legs. 'He'll be off work for months and just at the start of the season.'

'He's finished,' said Mr. Barlow less kindly. 'Waste of money messing about all summer and then pole-axing him in the autumn when we'd get the same price from the knacker now.'

'A grand old horse,' said Mr. Chandler mournfully. I felt so poorly that the thought of the knacker didn't bother me overmuch but my masters continued to argue.

Then Mr. Chandler had an idea. 'Let Biggs have him. If the sea water does the trick we'll get a sound horse back in the autumn if it doesn't, well, we don't stand to lose. He wrote yesterday asking if we had another crock for him this summer.'

'This one's a crock all right. I doubt you'll patch him up enough to get him to the sea. And what's more, is he broke to harness? Biggs won't be pleased to have his bathing machines kicked to pieces.'

CHAPTER TWELVE

A reunion

Mr. Chandler had won. After a few days in the stable I was led to the infirmary and there shod with a high-heeled shoe to relieve the pain of my old tendon trouble. I wasn't sound, but I could walk without too much pain and presently Mr. Biggs was brought by Mr. Chandler to see me. He was quite an old man, shabbily dressed and with a shapeless face, but he had a very pleasant voice and he obviously liked horses.

The first thing they did was to slip off my headstall and hold the collar from a set of harness out to me. I remembered the old days at Farmer Grey's and how I'd hated harness in my fierce determination to be a hunter.

But now it was harness or the knacker's and as the pain in my legs grew less I had begun to find some pleasure in life again, so I obediently thrust my head through the collar. This told them that I had been broken to harness. Mr. Chandler was all smiles. 'There, that's all right then. And you won't have any trouble with him; a kind old horse, a perfect gentleman, a general favourite.'

'You think he'll stand the work?' asked Mr. Biggs looking at my legs.

'A week of sea water and you won't know him,' answered Mr. Chandler confidently.

So Mr. Biggs and I set off for the sea. I'd always heard that train fares were expensive and now it seemed that my worth as an old crock was less than the fare, so we walked. It was early summer and the weather was kind to us. Mr. Biggs wasn't very talkative, but he was a tranquil and good-humoured companion. When we stopped for water and he gave me my nosebag and settled down to his own bread and cheese, I had the impression that he had done this walk many times before.

We were some distance out of London when we met a worried looking man with a red flag. ''Ang on to the 'orse for Gawd's sake!' he called, 'There's a motor car a-coming.'

And there it was, moving along in a very eerie way just as if a carriage had set off on its own without horses to pull it. I gave a snort, but, used as I was to trains and the noisy machinery of the colliery, I didn't shy or bolt or fall in the ditch as was expected.

'Nasty things,' said Mr. Biggs when it had passed. 'And they've gone on and on till they've got the law changed and they'll be going at fourteen miles an hour instead of four this summer and not even a red flag to warn you. The roads 'll be a death trap to horses.'

We spent the night at a farm and went on again next day. I was already feeling better. The new sights, the fresh country air and a good companion had all combined to raise my spirits and though my special shoe forced me to limp, I carried my head higher.

Towards evening the smell on the breeze changed. It no longer carried the sweetness of grass and trees, but had a sharp salty taste to it. Presently we stopped on a hill top and looked down to a vast expanse of grey blue water.

'Well, there's the sea for you, Ebony,' said Mr. Biggs. 'Don't know whether you've met up with it before.'

I followed him down a lane between cottages and we came to a field on a cliff. There was a broken down shed with a good bed of straw for me to sleep in. It wouldn't have done for a clipped horse, but I had grown my summer coat and except that I had been too well groomed and had no grease in my coat to protect me from the rain, I could have been turned straight out.

I liked my field, the grass was good and I enjoyed the freedom of pleasing myself, of going in and out of my shed and across to the water trough after so many years of standing in the stable and waiting for food and water to be brought to me.

There were birds and rabbits about, but I longed for a horse companion. There seemed to be plenty of donkeys nearby and when Mr. Biggs heard me answering their morning brays and realised that I was lonely he arranged for one to come and live with me.

Moses was his name. He said that a great crowd of donkeys was being collected to give rides on the beach to the holiday makers. He'd done it before and said it was not much of a job. The big boys tried to make you gallop, the stout trippers screamed and bounced about on your back, which was quite painful when they were so large and heavy. And you were expected to toil for long hours on hot days; he prefered the winter when he worked on a farm.

After I had rested for about two weeks, Mr. Biggs came into the field one day with a set of harness. It was old and mended but he'd kept it well oiled and he fitted it on me carefully. We went down to the shore, past the smoky houses and on to the sand, for the tide was out. Mr. Biggs who was wearing fisherman's boots, walked me along the edge of the sea and let the small waves lap round my hoofs. Gradually we went in deeper and deeper. I enjoyed splashing about.

Then we walked up the beach to where four little huts on wheels stood under the cliff. They all had shafts and a little platform in front, steps down at the back and a little window on either side. Mr. Biggs backed me between the shafts of one and hitched my traces to the hooks. Then he led me forward.

I had forgotten what hard work it is to get a vehicle started; you really have to throw yourself into the collar and pull with all your strength. Once they were moving those bathing machines were not too bad, unless their wheels sank into a soft patch of sand.

When we had got going Mr. Biggs climbed up on the platform and drove me in and out of the sea several times. Then he made a great fuss of me and took me back to my field and my leisured life. Another day I was taken to the forge and had a shoe with a less high-heel fitted and after that he would put on my driving bridle with a rope rein and ride me bare-back along the beach and into the sea almost every morning.

The days grew hotter and the season started. Moses left me to give his donkey rides and I pulled the four bathing machines along to the main beach, close to the pier and just below the hotels and the elegant villas where the summer visitors stayed. Mr. Biggs put out a large freshly-painted notice:

BATHING MACHINES FOR HIRE
Prop. E. BIGGS

The visitors were everywhere. Ladies with parasols, nurses carrying babies; little boys in sailor suits and little girls in print dresses and sun bonnets, pulling off their shoes and stockings and running to paddle in the sea. When the tides were right we spent a lot of time on that beach. Mr. Biggs wore his panama hat and I had a fringe on my browband to keep the flies from my eyes and a cotton rug to go over me when, waiting for customers, I stood dozing, tied to a ring in the sea wall.

There seemed to be special times for ladies and gentlemen to bathe and they were not allowed to mix, except for little boys who might go with either their fathers or their mothers.

When they had hired one of our machines they would climb in and change into their bathing costumes, meanwhile Mr. Biggs would put me in the shafts.

Then, when they were ready, he would jump on the platform or on my back and we would take the machine out into the water and turn it round so that the steps led directly down into the waves. I soon learned the routine and directly Mr. Biggs shouted 'whoa' I would stand, while he ran round to make sure that the steps were safe and that a rope or two was dangling down from the roof into the water, this gave the bathers something to hold on to and made them feel safe. Then he would unhitch me and sometimes we had to hurry for another customer would be waiting to be drawn up or down.

When we had all our four machines in a neat line along the water's edge, I would take a rest until they wished to be brought up but sometimes, if the tide was coming in, we would have a great rush to get them all up before they began to float.

On wet days I stayed in my shed and on Sundays there was no bathing and everyone went to church instead, so I had a day of rest in my field. Mr. Biggs fed me well and did not expect me to live on grass alone and the sea water strengthened my legs as Mr. Chandler had said it would. I began to feel younger, to carry my head high and to enjoy all the company. Some of the children would come to see me every day with an apple or lump of sugar and be quite sad when their holidays ended and we could meet no more.

Then, one hot August day when we were very busy, I heard a voice ask politely if there was a machine for hire.

'Certainly M'am. Just one moment and I'll be with you,' answered Mr. Biggs and, as we took the machine I was harnessed to into the sea, I thought about that familiar voice.

When we went back for the next machine I took a good look at the lady. Long pretty dress, hat, parasol, she was accompanied by a small boy and girl called Charlie and Katie. They looked just like all the other families on the beach, but each time the lady spoke I became more convinced that it was Miss Fanny. Dear Miss Fanny from my happy hunting days at Earleigh Court.

BIGGS

At first the children were too excited by the prospect of bathing to notice the horse, but afterwards they came round to pat me as Miss Fanny was paying for the hire. She called to them to be careful, for I was a strange horse and did not know them, but I could hear Mr. Biggs assuring her that I was very fond of children and perfectly safe.

Presently she came to fetch the children who didn't want to leave me. 'Oh what a dear old horse,' she said as I looked into her face with pricked ears. 'But he looks too well-bred for this sort of work.' Mr. Biggs began to explain about my accident and the excellent effect of salt water and I took Miss Fanny's cuff in my teeth and gave it a playful tug. Suddenly she sensed that I knew her. She turned to Mr. Biggs and asked in a strange voice if he knew my name or where I had been before the jobmaster.

'Ebony,' he said. 'And he answers to it, so he's had it a fairish time. And Mr. Chandler bought him from some sort of circus that had come down from the north.'

'Then it is Ebony, my old Ebony,' she said putting her arms round my neck and bursting into tears. The children and Mr. Biggs all looked horrified so she tried to explain.

'I've often told you of Ebony, the beautiful, black hunter I had when I was young, well I'm certain this is *my* Ebony, look, he knows me.'

I wished I could speak and tell her everything but, as I couldn't I put up my face and gave her the kiss I used to give Dick Turpin before I died. That made her cry the more.

'Don't take on so, M'am, you can see he's fit and

well and though he has come down in the world you can tell he has been kindly used, for a nicer-natured horse to handle you'd never find.'

Then Miss Fanny dried her eyes, and apologised for her tears. She gave me a loving pat saying that they would come back next day.

And next day she came again and brought her husband, Mr. Cavendish. He patted me and asked Mr. Biggs if there would be any possibility of buying me when the season was over. Mr. Biggs was very helpful. He explained that I belonged to Chandler and Barlow, and that his interest in me was only until the thirtieth of September, but that he was sure that they would accept any reasonable offer. Mr. Cavendish wrote down the London address.

So, by the time their holiday came to an end, Mrs. Fanny was able to tell me that it was all settled, that I was to be her's from October the first.

Mr. Biggs seemed very pleased. 'You've fallen on your feet, Ebony, and no mistake,' he said when they had gone. 'You'll be thoroughly petted and spoiled there; it'll suit you a lot better than riding school work.'

So the summer ended. I was quite sorrowful at parting with Mr. Biggs at the railway station, but I was very happy indeed when at the end of the journey I was led out of the train and found all the Cavendishes waiting for me on the station platform. They had brought their young groom, Sidney, and he was to ride me home while they went in the motor car driven by Mr. Cavendish.

The Paddocks wasn't a large establishment like Earleigh Court, but it looked a very comfortable sort of house set in its own meadows and orchards. The stables were near the house and very nice, for all the stalls had been made into loose boxes. Mr. Cavendish kept a hunter, Starchaser, and there were two ponies, Dandy and Dumpling. I was to carry Mrs. Fanny who had not been riding since she had the children. There were no carriage horses, for the motor car, which lived in the coach house, served instead, but there was a governess cart for the ponies.

It is a very happy home, Sidney is a cheerful groom and Mrs. Fanny is very pleased with me. She says that we have both grown old and must take things steadily and not as we did in our wild young days, but we have some very interesting times. The children have become fond of me, especially since they learned I can do tricks, though I won't 'die' for them very often as my joints are too stiff to be constantly getting up and lying down.

Charlie, like his father, is very attached to the motor car, and he and Katie are always dressing up as motorists in goggles and veils, huge caps and hats and long coats down to their feet; but they have often told me that they love horses best and me best of all the horses in the world.

If you've enjoyed reading this book, why don't you try some of the other stories about horses and riding available in Knight Books? Here and on the pages following are some of our suggestions:

Helen Griffiths

STALLION OF THE SANDS

The beautiful wild albino stallion who roamed the fog-bound Atlantic shores had become a legend to the gauchos, a ghost-horse. Yet Aurelio, the orphan boy who had joined the tough gaucho band, was determined to find the horse – and to tame him. It was said that the one who succeeded in capturing and riding the sand stallion would be the most 'gaucho' of them all, and for Aurelio, recently dishonoured in the eyes of the band, it was a challenge too strong to resist.

Judith Berrisford

A PONY IN THE FAMILY

Jane and Penny wanted to have a pony of their very own. When their father buys Freckles for them, they learn – often the hard way – how to feed, groom and look after her, as well as cope with a variety of pony emergencies. They also learn about the cost of keeping a pony . . . and prepare for their first gymkhana!

A COLT IN THE FAMILY

'Mishap, trouble, near disaster!' A farm tractor, a motor bike, a barking dog, the canal lock gates – all terrify the pony. But Jane and Penny Brooke are determined to train the unbroken colt, with Madge's help. But Rusty's fault is hard to cure. Will he ever be a safe pony?

A SHOW JUMPER IN THE FAMILY

Jane and Penny were dismayed when their father told them they weren't to show jump their ponies. Rusty, Penny's pony, had enormous potential and Penny just *knew* she mustn't spoil his chances. But it looked as if her hopes would come to nothing. Would she ever be able to prove Rusty's ability at the big local show?

Patricia Leitch

CROSS-COUNTRY PONY

Jinty and Nick decide to spend their summer holidays organising a pets' home, and their first resident is the pony Harold. Harold is ugly and has the habit of bucking. By accident Jinty discovers he is a marvellous jumper and cross-country galloper, but in the local show Harold lets Jinty down in the games and the jumping. Jinty and Nick have other troublesome and exciting residents at their pets' holiday home in this thrilling story.

A PONY OF OUR OWN

'We're a standing joke with everyone: "The Donaldsons, who are desperate to ride, haven't a horse, and when they do manage to borrow one, are too feeble to stay on." '

But perhaps the jokes would stop now, for at last Jean and her brother Stuart had saved up enough to buy a pony of their own. Jean dreamed of a neat grey or a dashing bay hunter.

But as it turned out, she was quite wrong.